One Potato, Two Potato

A Cookbook

by Constance Bollen and Marlene Blessing

Pacific Search Press

In memory of our paternal grandparents,
Harry and Myrtle Bollen and
Cliff and Maggie Loop

Pacific Search Press, 222 Dexter Avenue North,
    Seattle, Washington 98109
© 1983 by Constance Bollen and Marlene Blessing
Printed in the United States of America

Edited by Deborah Easter
Designed by Judy Petry
Illustrations by Constance Bollen
Cover photograph by Fred Milkie

Library of Congress Cataloging in Publication Data

Bollen, Constance, 1948-
    One potato, two potato.

    Includes index.
    1. Cookery (Potatoes) I. Blessing, Marlene,
1947-   . II. Title.
TX803.P8B57   1983   641.6'521   83-13243
ISBN 0-914718-82-7

Contents

Preface

We began our plans to write a cookbook, not knowing what kind of focus that book would have. Both of us are food lovers and amateur cooks who have reputations for cooking memorable meals for friends in our own homes. We wanted to compile recipes we had either invented or adapted or simply adopted that would be easy to prepare, even for an unseasoned cook, delicious to eat, and economical to serve. Surely, there were many routes to approach this aim. What evolved was our *One Potato, Two Potato* cookbook.

Potatoes are returning to the ranks of the special, the appreciated—and for good reason. They are available in favorite local varieties almost everywhere, they are the perfect accompaniment to any meat, fish, or poultry entrée (and are a vegetarian's delight), and they are a nutritional gold mine. Not only can a single potato provide 50 percent of your minimum daily requirement of vitamin C, but the potato also has important trace amounts of protein, iron, thiamine, and niacin.

Thanks in part to Jane Brody's popular nutrition guides, more and more people are aware of the potato's low-fat, low-calorie profile. Nevermore should we quake at the thought of complex carbohydrates in the form of something so comforting, so familiar as potatoes.

Which really leads us back to the inspiration for this book. We love to cook, to discover new ways to prepare familiar as well as exotic foods, and we wanted very much to collaborate on a project as a way of sharing our enthusiasms with other cooks and as a way of deepening our friendship with each other. Food *is* such a lovely medium of exchange.

For the taste for well-prepared garden vegetables, we can both credit our paternal grandparents for having provided us with the freshest, most carefully and wisely homegrown vegetables that any child could have had. I still hoard the memory of Grandpa Loop's buckets of fresh smelt or gleaming steelhead, accompanied by burlap sacks full of his favorite beans, carrots, potatoes, or strawberries and plums. For Constance, there is the vivid recollection of gathering button-size new potatoes from her grandparents' Lopez Island garden and tasting Grandma Bollen's new potatoes with fresh peas in cream sauce. These were simple pleasures, simple foods, but definitely the kind of country fare potatoes were central to.

We hope this collection of recipes will not only serve as a tribute to the potato and to our grandparents, but will also trigger some happy memory of the familiar pleasure of potatoes and will create new dining delights.

Introduction

History

Most of us have a personal history with the potato that dates back to the days when we were just learning to utter full sentences. But the potato predates our own memories by at least a few thousand years. The earliest record of man's cultivation of the potato goes back to about 3000 B.C., when the tribes that inhabited the cold and lofty climes of South America's Andes were carefully gathering hundreds of varieties of small, wild potatoes. Little wonder that these Indians dedicated ceremonies and objects of worship to this sturdy, edible tuber, certainly the hardiest and most reliable plant to grow at such an altitude.

The first European explorer to come into contact with this exclusively New World plant was Francisco Pizarro in the 1530s. If only he and his men had known that this knobby little plant would far surpass the riches to be found in gold and silver. But if the glamour of the potato escaped Pizarro's notice, it was not to be overlooked by the Old World forever.

Spain was the first country to embrace the potato. *Embrace* may be too hyperbolic, because there, as elsewhere, the underground, tuberous nature of the potato aroused peasant superstitions. After all, this was the first cultivated crop that was not grown from seed and that reached maturity underground—surely the devil's work. In fact, this bulbous, lumpen vegetable was blamed for a host of ills from leprosy, syphilis, consumption, and scrofula to hermaphroditism—a hefty list of charges that even prompted distressed peasantry to formally try and burn the potato at the stake.

Several European rulers grasped the importance of the potato, with its capacity to thrive in less than ideal environments, to yield twice as much food in a given field as grain crops, and to solve the hunger problem that plagued their subjects. And if the superstitious peasantry was resistant to this economic argument, the monarchies had novel ways to convince them. In Prussia in 1651, Frederick William I threatened to lop off the ears and noses of all who refused to cultivate the potato. In France, an eighteenth-century pharmacist named Antoine-Auguste Parmentier had a subtler solution. He persuaded Louis XVI to allow him to plant potatoes in Les Sablons, a sandy, barren field outside of Paris. As the potatoes grew and thrived, Parmentier further persuaded the king to post soldiers who guarded the fields by day and withdrew by night. Thinking these crops must be rare and valuable, the local peasants crept into the fields by night, stole the strange tubers, and began wide-scale cultivation.

By the eighteenth century, the masses had accepted the potato, even Russian peasants who claimed that it was un-Christian and sexually unclean because it reproduced by budding rather than by sexual fertilization. Having overcome these fears, the Irish were definitely the potato's greatest enthusiasts. Their country's thin, rocky soil and cold, wet climate proved ideal for the plant—so ideal that the potato eventually replaced most other crops. Potato yields were so successful that the population skyrocketed to about eight million Irish, more than double today's population. All this expansion and prosperity came to an abrupt halt, however, when a potato blight hit in 1845. It caused enormous crop losses and brought with it six years of famine and about one million deaths. Another million Irish fled to America in this period, as did successive generations of Irish citizens.

In spite of this dramatic setback, the potato continued to be a major European food crop. Potato production was a primary factor leading to a food surplus. The abundance of food, in turn, triggered a population explosion that made possible Europe's industrial growth. Even today, potatoes are the third largest food crop produced in the world, with half that crop going to feed livestock. These are the kinds of statistics that make eyeballs roll and heads nod in agricultural circles. What it means for someone who simply likes to eat potatoes is that they are readily available year-round and are inexpensive.

America's romance with the potato was fueled by Benjamin Franklin, who had been feted by Parmentier in France with an all-potato banquet, and later by Thomas Jefferson, that dedicated agrarian, who served the first french fries in the White House. What Americans found themselves heir to, in addition to a well-fed industrial revolution, was a wealth of potato dishes from all parts of Europe. Under the influence of Parmentier, the French gave America many of her favorite potato dishes: soufflé potatoes, potatoes au gratin, pureed potatoes, french fries, and potato soups. From the English, who under the influence of Elizabeth I had long regarded the potato as strictly an ornamental plant, America has the boiled potato and shepherd's pie. Americans have their own repertoire of potato cuisine, from the familiar hashed-brown potatoes, to home fries, to stuffed baked potatoes, and, of course, "Saratoga chips" or potato chips.

These are just a few possibilities. Because the potato is such an international favorite, our recipes include many variations on these dishes as well as many not mentioned here. We have continued to be surprised and pleased that, in the course of our recipe testing, we have not begun to exhaust the ways in which the potato can be prepared.

Nutrition Profile

Contrary to popular belief, the potato is a relatively low-calorie food that is perfectly suitable for weight watchers. A five-ounce potato, for example, has only 110 calories (that is, before we drown it in sour cream, butter, and bacon bits). Additionally, potatoes provide complex carbohydrates that will satisfy appetites better than calorie-dense fats and sweets.

Clearing away misinformation about how the potato is fattening is certainly a step in the direction of more balanced nutrition. Since the turn of the century, Americans have increasingly reduced their intake of carbohydrates, particularly foods such as flour, cereal grains, and potatoes. These are all foods that have been regarded as "low-prestige," the only source of nourishment for low-income families. Fortunately, the public is turning more and more to fresh pasta, granola, potatoes, and other sources of complex carbohydrates, once again demonstrating just how central a foodstuff the potato can be.

The most persuasive information we can find for reinstating the potato in our diets (beyond the sheer good taste of it) is its rich lode of vitamins and minerals. The profile of minimum daily requirements provided by the potato is something like this: 5 percent protein, 5 percent iron, 8 percent phosphorus, 10 percent thiamine, 11 percent niacin, and a whopping 50 percent vitamin C. For that matter, a person can derive nearly all necessary nutrients from a diet of nothing but potatoes. We would never, of course, recommend that regime to anyone but a determined *Guinness Book of Records* hopeful. We do, however, recommend making potatoes a cherished and regular element of your daily fare.

Potato Varieties and Their Uses

The four basic kinds of potatoes that you will encounter at your grocery store or public market are small red potatoes, russets, Finnish and Swedish (or yellow) potatoes, and white rose potatoes. New potatoes are not a separate variety but rather any potato dug before the vine dies down. These have a softer skin than later potatoes do and are often prized for such dishes as steamed new potatoes with butter and parsley.

We prefer referring to these various kinds of potatoes as either mealy or waxy, probably the most useful distinctions for determining how best to use them. Russets are the most popular mealy potatoes and are good for baking, mashed potatoes, and soups (especially purees). The small reds, yellow potatoes, and white rose potatoes are waxy—in other words, they have more liquid in their tissues and therefore retain their shape and do not absorb too much liquid or sauce. They are especially good for any kind of salad or gratin. But you can use any kind of potato you want in most of the recipes we have provided (with the exception of baked goods that require mealy potatoes). Just remember that the results will vary dramatically. For example, a chowder made with waxy potatoes will not break down into a comfortable mush—the kind that many people identify with homemade chowder. And a salad made with mealy potatoes will absorb most of the dressing and will break down more readily when tossed.

Buying and Storing

Be sure the potatoes you choose are firm, without cuts or bruises, and free of sprouts. Additionally, pick those that are relatively smooth and with only a few eyes and avoid those that have some greenish coloration. The green results from exposure to light and can make a potato taste bitter.

Storage is a good option for any kind of potato except new potatoes. They should be used within a week to ten days of purchase because they do not store well. Other kinds of potatoes can be stored for as long as several months. To do this, you will need a cool, dark, dry place at about forty-five to fifty degrees Fahrenheit. If you store them at seventy to eighty degrees, these same potatoes will keep for only a week. Storing them at a temperature below forty degrees will cause some of the potato's starch to turn to sugar, which spoils its flavor. You can reverse this process by simply letting the potatoes stand at room temperature for several days. The sugars will convert back to starch and the resulting chemical composition of the potato will approximate what it was when the potato was first dug.

Freezing is not a good way to store potatoes. Raw potatoes soften when frozen and cooked potatoes become grainy and mushy if frozen in liquid (a good reason to omit them from stews or casseroles you plan to freeze). You can, however, effectively freeze mashed and stuffed potatoes. Just be careful to mash them without allowing too much air into the mixture. (Don't whip them too long.) French fries and fried potato puffs are also fine candidates for freezing: simply reheat them in a 350-degree oven on a cookie sheet.

Basic Cooking Techniques

Before we describe how to cook potatoes, we would like to urge you to either bake or boil your potatoes in their skins. Potatoes baked in their skins retain most of their nutrients, and those boiled in their skins have less significant nutrient loss than those that have been pared and cut up. The more a vegetable is cut up before cooking, the greater the vitamin loss. So bearing that in mind, here are the simple techniques.

Boiling. You can either steam potatoes in a small amount of boiling salted water in a tightly covered, heavy saucepan or boil them in salted water to cover in a heavy saucepan. When tender, drain and place the potatoes over the heat for a few moments to dry out. The amount of time required to completely cook the potatoes will depend on the size of the potatoes and the number you have placed in a single pan. The best test is simply to poke the potatoes with fork tines periodically until they are tender.

Baking. Russets are the best potatoes for baking. Scrub the skins of the potatoes and either prick the skins with a fork and bake at 375 degrees for one hour or oil or butter the skins, then slit them about one-half inch deep and bake at 375 degrees for one hour. Again, time will vary depending on the size of the potatoes, so be sure to smell and poke to determine tenderness.

Salads_____

Salat Olivier
Serves 6 to 8

This is a sumptuous dish. During the days of czarist Russia, this salad was often among the elaborate array of dishes found in the zakuska *or hors d'oeuvres. Caviar, fish with sauces, pâtés, game, smoked meats with abundant condiments, fruits and vegetables in decorative salads, breads, and a full assortment of vodkas, all exquisitely served, created a formidable and artful first course. If you are feeling less ambitious than the czars' chefs, try this modified version for a wonderful brunch or dinner dish.*

Chicken breasts   2 whole, about ¾ pound each
Large onion   1, quartered
Salt   2 teaspoons
Dill pickles   ½ cup drained and chopped
Medium new potatoes   4, boiled, cooled, peeled, and sliced
Hard-cooked eggs   3, peeled and sliced
Mayonnaise (see Index)   ¾ cup
Sour cream   ¾ cup
Capers   1 to 2 tablespoons drained
Fresh dill   1 tablespoon finely chopped or
     Dried dill   1 teaspoon
Green olives   6, sliced
Pepper   to taste
Lettuce   1 head, leaves separated, washed, and patted dry (optional)
Medium tomato   1, peeled and cut into lengthwise slices (optional)

1. Combine chicken, onion, and 1 teaspoon salt in a large kettle with sufficient water to cover. Bring to a boil, skim fat, reduce heat, and simmer 10 to 15 minutes, until chicken is tender. Set aside to cool.
2. Combine pickles, sliced potatoes, and eggs in a large mixing bowl.
3. Remove and discard skin and bones from chicken meat. Cut into ½-inch chunks and add to potato mixture.
4. Blend mayonnaise and sour cream in small bowl. Add capers, dill, and olives and mix well. Pour into salad, blend and season with pepper.
5. Serve on bed of lettuce leaves, surrounded by tomato slices.

Note: For serving in the traditional Russian manner, add only half of the mayonnaise–sour cream mixture to salad, reserving olives, capers, and dill. Cover a serving platter with lettuce leaves and mound salad into the center, masking with remaining mayonnaise–sour cream mixture. Sprinkle with capers and dill and surround with whole olives and tomato slices.

Pesto Potato Salad*
Serves 4

Combining potatoes with pesto, a traditional Italian sauce, makes for a rich and interesting blend of flavors—a tempting departure from American-style potato salads.

Small garlic cloves 2, minced
Parmesan cheese ½ cup cubed or grated
Fresh basil leaves 2 cups or
    Fresh spinach leaves 2 cups plus
    Dried basil 1½ tablespoons
Pine nuts ¼ cup
Salt ½ teaspoon
Vegetable oil and olive oil ¼ cup each
Medium new red potatoes 3 to 4, boiled until just tender

1. Mince garlic and cheese in blender or processor. Add basil, pine nuts, and salt and process.
2. Gradually add oil until mixture has a smooth consistency. Transfer mixture to salad bowl.
3. Peel and slice potatoes, add to pesto, and toss lightly. Serve warm or at room temperature.

* Pesto will keep well for up to 1 week. Run a film of olive oil over the top, cover, and refrigerate. It can also be frozen. You can purchase prepared pesto fresh in some food specialty shops, but you can easily make it with blender, food processor, or with mortar and pestle.

Sausage and Potato Salad
Serves 4

Sausage salads are a staple of central European cuisine and this recipe will show you why.

Cooked sausage* ¾ pound, sliced or cubed
Medium potatoes 3, boiled, peeled, and sliced
Large tomato 1, chopped or
    Cherry tomatoes 8, halved
Green onions 4, thinly sliced
Olive oil 4 tablespoons
Red wine vinegar 1 tablespoon
German or dijon mustard 1 teaspoon
Parsley 2 tablespoons finely chopped

1. Place sausage, potatoes, tomatoes, and green onions in mixing bowl. Set aside.
2. Combine oil and vinegar, mustard, and parsley until frothy. Pour over potato mixture and toss well, careful not to break potato slices.
3. Chill for about 1 hour to marinate. Serve chilled or at room temperature.
*   Any cooked sausage is suitable, including frankfurters.

Mediterranean Potato Salad
Serves 4

This is an enticing potato salad, full of colorful, zesty ingredients.

Medium potatoes 4, boiled, peeled, and chilled
Green onions 3, chopped
Medium tomato 1, chopped
Ripe olives 8, pitted and chopped
Pimiento 2 tablespoons chopped
Mayonnaise ⅓ cup
Sour cream 2 to 3 tablespoons
Anchovy fillets 3, chopped
Capers 1 to 2 teaspoons, to taste

1. Slice chilled potatoes and place in mixing bowl. Add onions, tomato, olives, and pimiento and toss together carefully.
2. Prepare mayonnaise. Blend mayonnaise and sour cream. Stir in anchovies and capers, mixing well. Fold into potato mixture and chill to let flavors combine. Serve chilled or at room temperature.

Mayonnaise
Makes 1 cup

This is simple to make and far superior to commercial mayonnaise. Better yet, this is really a foolproof recipe.

Large egg   1 or
   Egg yolks   3
Dijon mustard   1 teaspoon
Wine vinegar or lemon juice   1 tablespoon
Salad oil   1 cup
Salt and pepper   to taste

1. In blender or food processor, process egg, mustard, and vinegar for 3 seconds to blend well.
2. With blender still running, add oil, a few drops at a time at first, then increasing to a slow, steady stream about $\frac{1}{16}$ inch wide. As you add oil, mayonnaise will thicken.
3. Taste and season with a few more drops of vinegar and salt and pepper, if desired.

Note: The key to making successful mayonnaise is to add the oil as slowly and evenly as possible. Also, part of the success of this recipe rests on your choosing a consistency and richness most pleasing to you. The whole egg mayonnaise is neither as stiff nor as rich as that made with egg yolks alone.

Creamy New Potato Salad
Serves 4 to 6

A luscious salad, with chopped walnuts and whipped cream dressing.

Medium new potatoes   3 to 4, boiled and cooled
Sweet red onion   ¼ cup chopped
Green pepper   ¼ to ½ cup chopped
Celery   ¼ to ½ cup chopped
Walnuts   ¼ cup chopped
Fresh dill   2 tablespoons chopped
Salt and pepper   to taste
Cream   ¼ cup
Mayonnaise (see Index) or sour cream   2 tablespoons

1.   Chop potatoes in their jackets. Add next 6 ingredients and toss carefully.
2.   Whip cream with mayonnaise and add to salad just before serving. Serve chilled or at room temperature.

Potato and Apple Salad
Serves 4 to 6

These flavors blend surprisingly well and make a pleasing sweet-tart salad.

Medium potatoes   4
Large Delicious (or other sweet) apples   2
Cider vinegar   2 tablespoons
Sugar   1 teaspoon
Celery   ½ cup diced
Pimiento   2 to 4 tablespoons chopped
Fresh chives or green onions   2 teaspoons minced
Salad oil   2 tablespoons
Mayonnaise (see Index)   ¼ cup

1.   Boil potatoes in their jackets until just tender. Peel and cut into ¼-inch slices when cool enough to handle.
2.   Quarter, core, and slice apples into ¼-inch slices. Pour vinegar and sugar over apples and toss well.
3.   Combine potatoes, apple mixture, celery, pimiento, and chives in large mixing bowl. Stir salad oil and mayonnaise together and pour over salad. Toss all ingredients and season to taste. Chill thoroughly before serving.

Ensaladilla Russa
Serves 4 to 6

This is one of our favorite salads. It is as good to look at as it is to taste.

Medium potatoes   2
Cooked peas   ½ cup
Cooked carrots   ½ cup diced
Pimiento   ¼ cup chopped
Onion   ¼ cup minced
Olive oil   2 tablespoons
Wine vinegar   2 tablespoons
Salt   ½ teaspoon
Pepper   to taste
Mayonnaise (see Index)   2 tablespoons

1. Boil potatoes in skins until tender. When cool, peel and cut into small dice, about ¼ inch.
2. Put potatoes in large bowl. Add peas, carrots, pimiento, and onion. Toss all ingredients thoroughly with oil, vinegar, salt, and pepper. Taste and correct seasoning.
3. Add mayonnaise (more or less according to taste) and toss again until everything is well combined. Chill well.

Note: To make this a centerpiece salad for guests, mound the salad carefully on an oval platter and shape it with the side of a knife until it is smooth and even. Spread mayonnaise over the salad until it is coated. Then decorate it with various garnishes such as parsley sprigs, carrot slices, slivers of red bell pepper, and chopped hard-cooked eggs.

Holiday Potato Salad
Serves 6 to 8

A delightful potpourri of flavors and textures, with each bite a special treat. This is great for potlucks or drop-in company over the Christmas holidays.

Mushrooms   ¼ pound, sliced
Mushroom Marinade
Medium waxy potatoes   6
Large tart green apples   2
Eggs   2, hard-cooked
Carrots   1 cup sliced
Medium dill pickles   4
Peas   1 cup barely cooked
Tiny pickled cocktail onions   ½ cup halved
Onion   1, finely chopped
Salt and pepper   to taste
Olive oil   2 tablespoons
Vinegar reserved from Mushroom Marinade   to taste
Mayonnaise Sauce
Red and green bell peppers   garnish
Radishes   garnish
Carrots   garnish
Parsley   garnish

1. Prepare mushrooms 1 day in advance by pouring marinade over them, covering, and setting aside for 24 hours.
2. Boil potatoes in jackets, cool, then dice. Quarter, core, and slice apples. Chop hard-cooked eggs and slice carrots.
3. Combine potatoes, apples, eggs, and carrots in giant mixing bowl and add pickles, peas, and pickled and fresh chopped onion.
4. Drain mushrooms, reserving marinade, and add to salad.
5. Season mixture with salt, freshly ground black pepper, olive oil, and a little of the marinade (being careful not to pour in the whole spices). Toss salad lightly to combine all ingredients. Taste and correct seasoning.
6. Add a few spoonfuls of Mayonnaise Sauce to salad and toss until

thoroughly blended. Be certain salad is correctly seasoned—it should not be bland.

7. Empty salad into large, attractive serving bowl. If size is correct, the salad should come almost to top of bowl when leveled. Smooth the top, pressing gently with a fork until it is as flat as possible. Spread remainder of sauce over it evenly.

8. Decorate with suggested colorful garnishes—or substitute your own favorites.

Mushroom Marinade

Cider Vinegar   ½ cup (or to cover)
Bay leaf   1
Pickling spice   1 teaspoon

1. Heat vinegar and seasonings.
2. Pour hot vinegar over mushrooms.

Mayonnaise Sauce

Egg yolks   3, hard-cooked
Olive oil   6 tablespoons
Lemon juice   3 tablespoons
Sugar   1 teaspoon
Sour cream   ¼ to ½ cup
Dijon mustard   1 tablespoon
Salt and pepper   to taste

1. Place egg yolks, olive oil, lemon juice, and sugar in blender and mix at high speed until oil emulsifies and mixture is smooth.
2. Add sour cream and mustard, along with salt and pepper, and blend again. (Sauce should be thick and pale yellow in color.)

Potato and Corned Beef Salad
Serves 4

This is a hearty, full-flavored salad that would be a meal in itself for Dinty Moore.

Corned beef   ¾ to 1 pound, cooked and thinly sliced
Medium potatoes   4, boiled and peeled
Medium beets   4, cooked or
    Canned beets   6
Dill pickle   1 to 2
Eggs   2, hard-cooked and sliced
Olive or salad oil   4 tablespoons
Wine vinegar   4 tablespoons
Dijon mustard   2 teaspoons
Chives or green onions   1 tablespoon chopped
Salt and pepper   to taste
Lettuce leaves   garnish (optional)
Hard-cooked eggs   garnish (optional)

1. Cut corned beef into ½-inch squares. Cut potatoes, beets, and pickle same size.
2. In salad bowl, combine corned beef, potatoes, beets, pickle, and eggs. Mix together oil, vinegar, mustard, and chives and add to salad. Salt to taste (remember that corned beef is already salty). Then add pepper.
3. Toss all ingredients thoroughly and let salad marinate in refrigerator at least 4 to 5 hours.
4. Line chilled dinner plates with lettuce leaves. Spoon salad onto lettuce leaves and garnish with additional wedges of egg.

Potato Salad with Sauce Verte and Greens Vinaigrette
Serves 4

Another variation on a favorite theme, this potato salad combines a pungent herb and caper sauce with refreshing, crisp greens.

Medium boiling potatoes   2 to 3, boiled
Dry white wine   3 tablespoons
Sauce Verte   ½ cup
Salt and pepper   to taste
Romaine lettuce leaves   8 to 10, washed and patted dry
Olive oil   2 tablespoons
Vegetable oil   1 tablespoon
Vinegar   2 teaspoons

1. Drain boiled potatoes. When cool enough to handle, peel and cut into ¼-inch slices. Toss gently with wine in a small bowl.
2. When wine has been absorbed, stir in Sauce Verte. Add salt and pepper to taste.
3. Just before serving, tear and toss greens with oils and vinegar. Arrange on a platter with potato salad in the center of bed of greens.

Sauce Verte
Makes 1 cup

This versatile, eggless sauce is made easily in a food processor or blender. It is foolproof and keeps well, if refrigerated, for a week.

Dijon mustard   3 tablespoons
Wine vinegar   1 tablespoon
Water   2 tablespoons
Olive oil and vegetable oil   ½ cup each
Evaporated milk   2 tablespoons, cold
Capers   1 to 2 teaspoons well drained
Parsley sprigs   6 to 8, washed and patted dry
Large fresh basil leaves   12 or
    Dried tarragon   1 teaspoon
Salt   ½ teaspoon
Pepper   to taste

1. Blend mustard, vinegar, and water in processor.
2. Add oils with machine running, a few drops at a time, alternating with drops of cold milk.
3. When all milk and oil have been added, scrape down sides of work bowl and add capers and herbs, processing until well chopped and blended. Season with salt and pepper.

Insalatone
Serves 6 to 8

This assortment of marinated cooked and raw vegetables or "insalatone" is good as antipasto or salad. It is a special treat during those late summer / early fall months when tomato growers have a surplus of green tomatoes.

Medium potatoes   3
Medium zucchini   2
Marinade
Celery hearts and/or stalks   1 cup sliced
Medium red tomatoes   2
Medium green tomatoes   2
Olive oil   ⅓ cup
White wine vinegar   ¼ cup
Parsley   3 tablespoons minced
Basil   ½ teaspoon crushed
Oregano   ½ teaspoon crushed
Salt and pepper   to taste

1. Boil potatoes in jackets until just tender. Drain and cool.
2. Trim and slice zucchini ¼ inch thick. Put slices in enameled pot with Marinade, using just enough water to cover zucchini completely. Bring to a boil; then lower heat slightly. Boil slices for exactly 5 minutes, remove with slotted spoon (reserving Marinade), and run cold water over them. Chill until needed.
3. Place celery slices in reserved Marinade, bring to a boil again, and cook for 8 to 10 minutes. Drain, run cold water over them, and chill until needed.
4. Peel potatoes, quarter lengthwise, and thickly slice. Quarter and slice tomatoes. Combine all vegetables in large bowl, add remaining ingredients, and toss gently until dressing is evenly distributed. Taste and correct seasoning.
5. Chill salad for at least 1 to 2 hours and toss once more before serving.

Marinade

Red wine vinegar   ⅔ cup
Olive oil   3 tablespoons
Water   about 1½ cups (to cover)
Salt   to taste

1. Combine all ingredients in an enameled skillet or pot.

New Potato and Prosciutto Salad
Serves 4

This is a tart (horseradish, dijon mustard, and lemon juice) and rich (sour cream, prosciutto, and gruyère) salad that surely ranks as one of the most luxurious of potato salads.

Small new potatoes 9
Sour cream ½ cup
Prepared horseradish 1 teaspoon
Dijon mustard ½ teaspoon
Small lemon juice of ½
Salt and pepper to taste
Prosciutto 2 ounces, chopped
Gruyère or swiss cheese ⅓ cup finely cubed
Celery stalk 1, thinly sliced
Parsley 2 tablespoons chopped

1. Drop potatoes into boiling salted water and reduce heat and simmer until just tender. Drain, dry, and let potatoes cool completely. (You may refrigerate at this point.) Cut potatoes into thin slices.
2. Combine sour cream, horseradish, mustard, lemon juice, salt, and pepper in large bowl and blend well. Add potato slices and toss to coat with dressing.
3. Gently stir in prosciutto, cheese, celery, and parsley. Cover and chill. Let stand at room temperature for approximately 30 minutes before serving.

Artichoke, Ham, and New Potato Salad
Serves 4

These ingredients combine for a simple, but superlative salad.

Medium new potatoes   3 to 4
Marinated artichoke hearts   6-ounce jar
Cooked ham   ¾ cup chopped
Chopped ripe olives   4.2-ounce can, well drained
Mayonnaise (see Index)   3 tablespoons

1. Boil potatoes in jackets in salted water until just tender. Drain. When cool enough to handle, slice. (Peel, if desired.)
2. Drain artichoke hearts, reserving 1 teaspoon of marinade. Chop hearts and combine with reserved marinade, ham, olives, and mayonnaise in mixing bowl.
3. Fold in potato slices and correct seasoning. Serve at room temperature or chilled.

German Hot Potato Salad
Serves 6

Although the Germans were among the last Europeans to accept the potato or kartoffel *as an edible, today it is the king of vegetables in Germany. The German people use potatoes in myriad ways, not the least of which is this traditional hot potato salad.*

Medium potatoes   6
Bacon strips   4, minced
Onion   ¼ cup chopped
Celery   ¼ cup chopped
Large dill pickle   1, chopped
Chicken stock or water   ¼ cup
Vinegar   ½ cup
Sugar   ½ teaspoon
Paprika   ⅛ teaspoon
Dry mustard   ¼ teaspoon
Salt   ½ teaspoon

1. Cook potatoes in their jackets in salted water to cover until tender. Remove from heat, drain, and peel and slice while hot.
2. Heat bacon strips in skillet. Add onion, celery, and pickle and sauté until brown.
3. Heat remaining ingredients in saucepan and pour into skillet when hot. Combine mixture with potatoes and serve.

Corned Beef, Potato, and Sauerkraut Salad
Serves 4 to 6

Another splendid buffet salad, rich and tangy and packed with meat.

Medium potatoes   3 to 4
Cream   ½ cup
Dusseldorf or dijon mustard   2 teaspoons
Wine vinegar   2 tablespoons
Salad oil   1 tablespoon
Mayonnaise (see Index)   ¼ cup
Corned beef   ½ to 1 pound deli-style, thinly sliced
Salt and pepper   to taste
Sauerkraut   1½ cups, thoroughly drained
Medium onion   1, quartered and thinly sliced
Sour cream   1 cup
Caraway seeds   2 teaspoons pounded in mortar to release aroma
Lettuce leaves   garnish (optional)

1. Boil potatoes in jackets in salted water until just tender. Peel while still warm and cut into slices that are ¼ inch thick and 1 inch in diameter.
2. In mixing bowl combine cream, mustard, vinegar, salad oil, and mayonnaise. Stir well with wire whisk. Add potato slices and stir to coat.
3. Cut corned beef into 1-inch squares and add to potato mixture. Toss thoroughly and season to taste. Lightly oil an 8½-inch ring mold and press mixture in tightly and chill at least 2 hours.
4. Combine drained sauerkraut, onion slices, sour cream, and caraway. Mix well and chill.
5. Unmold corned beef mixture on a platter, garnished with lettuce leaves if desired. Spoon sauerkraut mixture into center and serve.

Arabic Potato Salad
Serves 4

Mint, parsley, and olive oil, though typical of the Middle East where this recipe originates, make a surprising, spunky salad for Western tastes.

Medium potatoes   4
Small onion   1, finely chopped
Parsley   ¼ to ½ cup chopped
Dried mint   ¼ teaspoon ground to powder
Salt and pepper   to taste
Garlic clove   1, minced
Salt   1 teaspoon
Lemon juice   ¼ cup
Olive oil   ¼ cup
Salt and pepper   to taste

1. Boil potatoes in jackets in salted water until tender. Peel and cut into cubes when cool.
2. Place potatoes in bowl, adding onion, parsley, mint, and salt and pepper to taste.
3. Crush garlic in separate bowl with salt and mix to a paste. Stir in remaining ingredients and beat thoroughly with a fork. Pour over potatoes and toss. Serve at room temperature.

Mom's Potato Salad
Serves 6 to 8

Everyone probably has a family classic when it comes to potato salad. It's the salad that is always at the family picnic and the Easter buffet. Somehow, when you're in a certain mood, nothing will do but "Mom's."

Medium potatoes*   6, boiled, peeled, and chopped
Small onion   1, chopped
Dill pickle   1 to 2, chopped
Hard-cooked eggs   2, chopped
Celery stalk   1, sliced (optional)
Radishes   2 to 3, sliced (optional)
Mayonnaise (see Index)   ½ to ¾ cup
Prepared mustard   2 to 3 teaspoons or to taste
Salt and pepper   to taste

1. Combine first 6 items in salad bowl.
2. Mix mayonnaise and mustard together and add to salad, blending well. Season and chill or serve at room temperature.

* All-purpose, russet-type potatoes are often used in this salad. They absorb more of the dressing than the waxier kind. Be careful not to overcook them, though, since they have a tendency to get mushy easily. If you prefer the texture of thin-skinned waxy potatoes, try to peel, chop, and combine them with the dressing while they are still warm from being cooked so that some of the dressing is absorbed.

Note: To have the most flavorful salad possible, allow for several hours of sitting time so the potatoes fully absorb the dressing.

Scandinavian Beet and Potato Salad
Serves 6

A lovely, colorful salad that is both sweet and spicy, smooth and crisp, all blended together in a fluffy whipped cream dressing.

Beets   1 to 1½ cups, cooked and sliced
Potatoes   1½ to 2 cups, cooked and sliced
Celery stalks   2, sliced
Small red onion   1, thinly sliced
Iceberg lettuce   ½ head, torn
Hard-cooked egg whites   2, shredded
Hard-cooked egg yolks   2
White vinegar   1 tablespoon
Sharp mustard   1 teaspoon
Raw egg yolk   1
Salt and pepper   to taste
Sugar   1 teaspoon
Whipped cream   1 cup (unsweetened)

1. Combine beets, potatoes, celery, onion, lettuce, and egg whites. Toss.
2. In another bowl, mash hard yolks with vinegar and mustard. Beat in raw yolk.
3. Add all remaining ingredients except whipped cream to yolk mixture. Fold in cream gently and toss with vegetables at the table.

Potato-Asparagus Salad
Serves 6

A delightful spring salad featuring fresh asparagus and watercress.

Medium new potatoes   2 to 3, boiled and sliced
Cooked asparagus   2 cups cut into 1-inch pieces
Hard-cooked eggs   3, sliced
Stuffed green olives   6, sliced (optional)
Watercress   1 bunch, cleaned and chopped
Sour cream   ½ cup
Mayonnaise (see Index)   2 to 3 tablespoons
Chives   2 teaspoons chopped
Lemon juice   2 to 3 tablespoons
Salt   to taste
Paprika   ¼ teaspoon
Curry powder   pinch

1. Combine potatoes, asparagus, eggs, and olives in a large mixing bowl and chill. Prepare watercress and chill separately.
2. Combine next 7 ingredients just before serving. Add watercress to potato mixture, pour dressing over, and toss lightly. Correct seasoning, adding more mayonnaise or lemon juice, if desired.

Potato Salad with Peas and Pearl Onions
Serves 6

A fresh, sweet-tart salad that is exceptionally easy to make.

Medium potatoes   3
Frozen peas with pearl onions   10-ounce package or
   Fresh peas and pearl onions   ¾ cup each
Egg yolks   3, well-beaten
Cream   ¾ cup
Dijon mustard   1 teaspoon
Dry mustard   ½ teaspoon
Butter   2 tablespoons
Sugar   1 tablespoon
Vinegar   ¼ cup
Salt and pepper   to taste

1. Boil potatoes in their jackets until just tender. Drain, let cool briefly, then cut into ½-inch cubes.
2. Cook peas and onions per package instructions, but for slightly less time. (For fresh peas and onions, parboil for several minutes until somewhat tender.) Drain and add to potatoes.
3. Combine egg yolks, cream, both mustards, butter, and sugar in top of double boiler. Cook over simmering water until sauce thickens, stirring often. Remove from heat and stir in vinegar; salt and pepper to taste.
4. Add dressing to potatoes, peas, and onions and toss well. Chill for several hours, but allow to return to room temperature before serving.

Potato Salad Niçoise
12 servings

A specialty of Nice in the south of France, this makes an excellent buffet or summertime luncheon dish.

Medium new potatoes 6 to 8
Garlic clove 1, peeled
White wine ½ cup, heated, or
    Wine vinegar and chicken stock ¼ cup each
Cucumber 1, peeled, seeded, and finely chopped (optional)
Whole cooked green beans 3 cups, chilled
Medium tomatoes 4 to 6, quartered
Olive oil 4 tablespoons
Wine vinegar 2 tablespoons
Mustard powder ¼ teaspoon
Salt and pepper to taste
Salad greens garnish
Capers 2 tablespoons
Small pitted black olives ½ cup
Anchovy fillets garnish (optional)
Tuna 7-ounce can, drained (optional)

1. Cook potatoes in water to which garlic clove has been added. Drain, peel, and slice and, while still warm, sprinkle with heated wine. Let stand at 70° for 1 hour.
2. When potatoes have cooled, toss with cucumber.
3. Marinate beans and tomatoes in a mixture of oil, 2 tablespoons wine vinegar, and mustard. Salt and pepper to taste.
4. To serve, mound potatoes in center of a platter garnished with salad greens. Garnish potatoes with capers, olives, and anchovies. Alternate tomato quarters and small heaps of green beans (and mounds of flaked tuna, if desired) around the potatoes.

Herring, Apple, and Potato Salad
Serves 4 to 6

Few salads can rival this one for variety of flavors and textures. It is a complete delicatessen in a bowl.

Potatoes   2 to 3 cups boiled and diced
Cooked or canned beets   1 cup drained and diced
Sweet red apples   2, cored and diced
Herring fillets (salted, spiced, or pickled)   6-ounce jar, chopped
Dill pickle   ½ cup chopped
Green onions   2 to 3 tablespoons chopped
Salad oil   6 tablespoons
Vinegar   2 tablespoons
Salt and pepper   to taste
Sour cream   ¼ to ½ cup (optional)

1. In a large salad bowl, combine potatoes, beets, apples, herring, dill pickle, and onion. Whisk salad oil and vinegar together and add to salad, blending well.
2. Cover and refrigerate for at least a day. Salt and pepper to taste, and fold in sour cream if desired. Serve chilled.

Potato and Green Vegetable Salad
Serves 4

A potato salad like this one provides plenty of crunch for those who like to feel the freshness of salad ingredients.

Medium potatoes   2, boiled, peeled, and diced
Parsley   ¼ cup chopped
Green beans   ½ cup cooked and chopped
Green pepper   ½ cup chopped
Celery stalks   2, sliced
Green onions   2, sliced (including some green)
Dill pickle   ¼ cup chopped
Tuna meat   ½ cup flaked (optional)
Mayonnaise (see Index)   6 tablespoons
Olive or vegetable oil   1 teaspoon
Vinegar   1 teaspoon
Dry mustard   ½ teaspoon
Salt and pepper   to taste

1. Mix vegetables and pickle together in large bowl. Add tuna if desired.
2. Combine mayonnaise, oil, vinegar, mustard, salt, and pepper. Fold into vegetable mixture and blend well. Chill before serving.

French Vegetable Salad
Serves 6 to 8

Ideal with hors d'oeuvres or as the salad course, this vegetable potpourri combines some of our favorite ingredients.

Medium new potatoes 4, diced
Medium carrots 2, diced
Fresh green beans 1 cup trimmed or
    Frozen green beans 9-ounce package
Small cauliflower ½ head, broken into small flowerets
Artichoke hearts 8½-ounce can, drained and quartered
Large cucumber 1, peeled, seeded, and diced
Salt and pepper ¼ teaspoon each
Garlic cloves 2, minced
Dry mustard ½ teaspoon (optional)
Olive oil ¾ cup
Wine vinegar or lemon juice ¼ cup
Salt and pepper to taste
Parsley 2 tablespoons chopped
Capers 2 tablespoons (optional)

1. Cook potatoes, carrots, and fresh green beans together in boiling salted water until tender but still firm (about 6 to 7 minutes).
2. Cook cauliflower (and frozen green beans, if used) separately until just tender. Drain and combine vegetables, adding artichoke hearts and diced cucumber. Set aside to cool slightly.
3. Combine ¼ teaspoon each salt and pepper with the garlic, mustard, and small amount of oil and vinegar; whip until blended. Add remaining oil and vinegar and mix thoroughly. Add to vegetable mixture and toss, seasoning with additional salt and pepper to taste.
4. Chill salad for at least 1 hour. Toss again, turn it out onto a platter, and garnish with parsley and capers.

Coburg Potato Salad
Serves 4 to 6

This recipe hails from Coburg, once an aspiring German duchy, now more a part of modern-day Bavaria. These few simple ingredients combine to make a surprisingly distinctive and delicious salad.

Potatoes   4 to 5
Beef stock   ¾ to 1 cup
Onion   ¾ to 1 cup minced
Vegetable oil   ¼ cup
White wine vinegar   3 tablespoons
Salt and pepper   to taste
Chives   garnish

1. Boil potatoes in their jackets until just tender. Drain them, return to pan, and shake over low heat until dry. When cool enough to handle, peel and thinly slice potatoes.
2. Warm beef broth. Combine it with onion, vegetable oil, vinegar, and salt and pepper in a large heat-proof bowl.
3. Add potatoes and toss gently. Sprinkle with fresh chopped chives. Serve warm or chilled.

Soups,
Stews,
and Chowders_____

Finnish Vegetable Soup
Serves 4 to 6

The success of this light, delicately flavored soup depends on using the freshest and sweetest vegetables available. Makes a wonderful summer luncheon or supper soup.

Small new potatoes   2 to 3, diced
Small carrots   2, diced
Fresh green peas   ½ cup shelled
Cauliflower   ½ to 1 cup cut into flowerets
String beans   ½ cup cut into small strips
Small red radishes   2 to 3, sliced
Spinach   1 cup washed, drained, and finely chopped
Salt   1 teaspoon
Butter   1 tablespoon
Flour   1 tablespoon
Milk   ½ cup
Egg yolk   1
Cream   ¼ cup
Cooked shrimp   ¼ to ½ cup (optional)
Salt and pepper   to taste
Parsley or fresh dill   ½ tablespoon chopped

1. Place all vegetables except for spinach in a 2- to 3-quart pot, with just enough water to cover. Add salt and boil uncovered for 5 minutes, or until vegetables are tender.
2. Add spinach and cook another 5 minutes. Remove pan from heat and strain liquid through a fine sieve into a bowl. Set vegetable stock and vegetables aside in separate bowls.
3. Melt 2 tablespoons butter in pan over moderate heat. Stir in flour and cook for about 2 minutes. Pour in hot vegetable stock, a small amount at a time, beating vigorously with a wire whisk; then beat in milk.
4. Combine egg yolk and cream in a small bowl. Whisk in 1 cup of hot soup, 2 tablespoons at a time. Now reverse process and slowly whisk warmed egg yolk and cream mixture back into soup.
5. Add reserved vegetables to soup and bring to a simmer. As soon as it comes almost to a boil, reduce heat, add cooked shrimp, and simmer uncovered over low heat for 3 to 5 minutes, or until shrimp and vegetables are heated through.
6. Taste and correct seasoning. Pour into a soup tureen and sprinkle with finely chopped parsley.

Potato and Watercress Soup
Serves 4

A rich and savory soup, which owes its distinctive flavor to the watercress.

Butter   4 tablespoons
Medium onion   1, chopped
Chicken stock   4 cups
Russet potato   1, chunked
Watercress leaves   2 to 3 cups, packed
Cream   1 cup
Eggs   2
Lemon juice   1 to 2 tablespoons
Sugar   1 teaspoon (optional)
Salt and pepper   to taste

1. Melt butter in a large pot and sauté onions in it until they just begin to turn golden.
2. Add stock and potato pieces, bring to a boil, reduce heat, and cook until potatoes are tender.
3. Add watercress and simmer soup for about 10 more minutes. In small batches, puree soup in a blender or processor until it is perfectly smooth. Return soup to pot.
4. Beat together cream and eggs and continue beating as you pour in about 2 cups of hot soup. Stir this mixture back into soup, off the heat. Season soup with lemon juice, sugar, salt, and pepper. Over moderate heat, stir soup for about 5 minutes, or until it is heated through (and egg white has set) but not boiling. Serve immediately.

German Potato Soup with Cucumber
Serves 4 to 6

A subtle, refreshing soup that manages to seem light in spite of its richness.

Medium boiling potatoes　4 to 5
Cold water　3 cups
Salt　1½ teaspoons
Pepper　to taste
Cream　1 cup
Milk　1 cup
Onion　1 to 2 tablespoons minced
Medium cucumber　1, peeled, seeded, and diced
Fresh dill　1 tablespoon chopped or
　　Dried dill　1 teaspoon

1.　In a heavy 3- to 4-quart saucepan, bring potatoes and water to a boil over high heat. Reduce heat to moderate. Add salt and pepper and cook uncovered until potatoes are very soft. Mash potatoes coarsely in their liquid.
2.　Stir in cream, milk, minced onion, and cucumber. Simmer over low heat for about 5 minutes, or until cucumber is tender but still somewhat firm. Add dill and taste for seasoning. Serve hot either from a heated tureen or in individual soup bowls.

Dutch Farmer's Soup
Serves 4 to 6

A comforting, thick vegetable soup topped with crumbled bacon.

Butter　3 tablespoons
Medium potatoes　2, peeled and diced
Medium carrots　2, chopped
Small cauliflower　½, cut into small flowerets
Medium onion　1, chopped
Chicken stock　3 cups
Bacon slices　5 to 6, cut into 1-inch pieces
Gouda cheese　½ cup grated

1. Melt butter in large saucepan. Add potatoes, carrots, cauliflower, and onion and sauté until onion is golden and vegetables are glazed, about 5 minutes.
2. Add stock and bring to boil. Reduce heat and let simmer 30 minutes.
3. Meanwhile, fry bacon until crisp. Drain on paper towels and set aside.
4. Stir in gouda cheese and heat until cheese melts. When ready to serve, ladle soup into tureen or serving bowls. Sprinkle with bacon.

C. B.'s Chicken Soup
Serves 4 to 6

This is one of those soups that has "evolved" over the years and has become famous among our family and friends. It reheats well for days (and seems to soothe sore throats, as well as winter blahs).

Small stewing chicken   2½ to 3 pounds or
    **Chicken backs and necks with one meaty piece (breast) added for
        last ½ hour**   2 pounds backs and necks plus 1 pound breast
Chicken stock   8 cups
Medium potatoes   4 to 5, cubed
Medium onions   2, chopped
Celery stalks   2 to 3, sliced
Mushrooms   ¼ to ½ pound, sliced
Butter   3 tablespoons
Parsley   2 tablespoons chopped
Flour   2 tablespoons
Cream or canned milk   1 cup

1. Simmer chicken in stock for about 1 hour, occasionally skimming fat. Remove chicken with slotted spoon to cool.
2. Add potatoes, onions, and celery to stock and simmer for 30 to 40 minutes until very tender.
3. While vegetables cook, sauté mushrooms in 1 tablespoon butter until browned. Set aside.
4. Bone and tear chicken meat into bite-sized chunks, discarding skins. Add chicken meat, mushrooms, and parsley to vegetables during last 10 to 15 minutes of cooking.
5. Make a roux with 2 tablespoons butter and flour, adding cream slowly until thickened. Slowly mix in about 1 cup of hot stock from soup, whisk together, and return to soup. Heat through until ingredients have blended and soup is hot but not boiling. Serve immediately.

Potato Soup
Serves 4 to 6

There are hundreds of wonderful potato soup recipes. The thing that distinguishes this one is the addition of sour cream—vive la différence!

Large russet potatoes   4, diced
Leeks   3 to 4, white part only, chopped
Water   3 to 4 cups (to cover)
Salt   to taste
Cream or milk   1 cup
Caraway seeds   ½ teaspoon
Dill weed   2 tablespoons
Salt   1 teaspoon
Pepper   to taste
Sour cream   ¼ to ½ cup
Butter   2 tablespoons
Chives   garnish

1.   Cook potatoes and leeks in salted water about 30 minutes, or until tender.
2.   Add cream, caraway seeds, dill, and salt and pepper to taste. Let soup simmer another 15 to 20 minutes, or until consistency is thick and potatoes begin to fall apart a little.
3.   Stir in sour cream and butter; heat through and serve, garnished with chopped chives.

Variation: For a richer soup with a milder taste, replace the water with chicken stock (or season water with bouillon to taste) and omit caraway, dill, and salt. Then add chopped parsley instead of chives before serving.

Potato-Asparagus Soup
Serves 3 to 5

Asparagus lovers will enjoy the strictly asparagus flavor of this soup, undisguised by elaborate seasonings, but enhanced by the body and "fluff" of potatoes.

Medium potatoes   2 to 3
Salted water   4½ cups
Asparagus   ¾ to 1 pound
Cream   ½ cup
Egg yolks   2
Butter   1 tablespoon
Salt and pepper   to taste

1. Boil potatoes in salted water until tender. Remove potatoes, reserving liquid. Set potatoes aside to cool.
2. Trim and chop asparagus and add to reserved cooking liquid. Simmer until tender.
3. Peel and chop potatoes and place in a blender or food processor, along with half of drained asparagus pieces. Add cream and egg yolks and process thoroughly. (Process in batches if necessary.)
4. Stir puree into broth with remaining asparagus pieces and butter. Simmer until soup is smooth and slightly thickened. Season with salt and pepper to taste and serve.

Potato and Spinach Soup
Serves 4

A refreshing combination of flavors makes this light soup delicious and satisfying. Serve hot or cold.

Chicken stock   1 quart
Green onions   ½ cup chopped
Fresh spinach   1 bunch, chopped or
   Frozen spinach   1 cup thawed
Medium large potatoes   2 to 3, diced
Salt and pepper   to taste
Sour cream   ½ cup
Lemon juice   1 to 1½ tablespoons, to taste
Sour cream   garnish (optional)

1. Heat stock in large pot or soup kettle. Add half of onions to pot, along with spinach and potatoes. Simmer with salt and pepper for about an hour, stirring occasionally.
2. Ladle out about 1 cup broth and whisk it with ½ cup sour cream. Return to soup and stir. Add 1 tablespoon lemon juice and remaining green onions and simmer gently for another hour.
3. Adjust seasoning with salt, pepper, and additional lemon juice, if desired. Serve hot or cold with dollops of sour cream.

Potato-Cheese Soup with Summer Sausage
Serves 4

The summer sausage and herbs in this soup give it a lively flavor. It is especially easy to make and is delicious reheated.

Russet potatoes   2 to 3
Small onion   1, sliced
Water   2 to 3 cups
Summer sausage   ½ cup diced
Thyme leaves   ½ teaspoon crushed
Marjoram leaves   ½ teaspoon crushed
Salt and pepper   to taste
Butter   2 tablespoons
Sharp cheddar cheese   ½ cup grated
Parmesan cheese   to taste (optional)

1. Quarter potatoes and combine and cook with onion in 2 cups boiling water until tender. Do not drain.
2. Mash potatoes and onions in their cooking liquid until fairly smooth. Add diced sausage, thyme, marjoram, salt, pepper, and butter. Stir in cheddar and enough additional boiling water to reach desired consistency. (Soup should not be watery.)
3. Simmer about 10 minutes more or until cheese is melted and flavors have blended. Serve with sprinkling of grated parmesan if desired.

Beef Soup with Vegetables and Apricots
Serves 6

Apricots are a familiar seasoning in Middle Eastern cooking, and this soup is a perfect introduction for the uninitiated.

Butter   4 tablespoons
Onion   ¼ cup finely chopped
Medium tomatoes   2, peeled, seeded, and coarsely chopped
Beef stock   1 quart
Waxy potatoes   2 cups peeled and cut into 1-inch cubes
Dried apricots   ¼ cup cut into quarters
Salt   1½ teaspoons
Pepper   ⅛ teaspoon
Boiled chuck or brisket of beef   1 pound, cut into 1-inch cubes
Fresh coriander   2 tablespoons

1. Melt butter over high heat in a heavy 10- to 12-inch skillet. Add onion and, stirring frequently, cook uncovered for 5 to 8 minutes, or until soft and lightly colored. Stir in tomatoes and boil briskly, uncovered, until most of liquid has evaporated and mixture has thickened slightly.
2. Stir in beef stock. Then add potatoes, apricots, salt, and pepper, and bring to a boil over high heat. Reduce heat to moderate, cover pan, and cook undisturbed for 20 minutes, or until potatoes are tender but not falling apart.
3. Stir in meat and simmer slowly for 10 minutes. Taste for seasoning. Transfer soup to large heated tureen or soup bowls, sprinkle with coriander, and serve at once.

Meat and Potato Borscht
Serves 4 to 6

This is the best hot borscht we've tasted, and with everything but the kitchen sink thrown in, it makes a hearty and satisfying meal by itself.

Beef stock   4 cups
Boneless beef chuck   1 pound, cut into 1-inch cubes
Medium potatoes   2, cut into ¾-inch cubes
Medium onion   1, chopped
Medium cooked beets   2 or
       Canned beets   10-ounce can, cut into strips, reserve liquid
Beet liquid   ½ cup
Medium carrots   2, quartered, cut into 1-inch strips
Butter   ½ cup
Green cabbage   1 cup shredded
Parsley   ½ cup chopped
Wine vinegar   1 to 2 tablespoons
Salt and pepper   to taste
Sour cream   1 cup or to taste
Dill or parsley   garnish

1. Simmer stock and beef cubes for 5 minutes in large, heavy pot.
2. Skim stock and add potatoes, onion, beets and their liquid, and carrots. Cover and simmer for 1½ hours.
3. Melt butter in a skillet and add cabbage and parsley. Sauté for 5 minutes and add to pot, along with vinegar and salt and pepper to taste. Cook for additional 30 minutes or until meat is tender. Serve hot, garnished with sour cream and dill.

Portuguese Potato, Greens, and Sausage Soup
Serves 4

This is a nutritious and gratifying soup. In Portugal, it is traditionally served with corn bread and a dry red table wine.

Polish sausage or other pork garlic sausage   6 to 8 ounces
Medium potatoes   3, sliced
Water   4 to 5 cups
Salt   1 teaspoon
Olive oil   ½ cup
Spinach, collard greens, or green lettuce   2 to 3 cups chopped
Salt and pepper   to taste

1. Pierce sausage in 3 places with a fork, cover with cold water, heat to boiling, simmer for 15 minutes, drain, and cut into ¼-inch slices.
2. Put potatoes in a heavy pot, cover with salted water, cover, and boil until potatoes are tender. Remove potatoes, mash until smooth, and return to pot.
3. Add oil and sausages and heat to boiling. Add greens and boil, uncovered, until tender, about 3 minutes. Season with salt and pepper to taste and serve piping hot.

Cream of Artichoke Soup
Serves 4 to 6

This hearty soup is an artichoke lover's delight.

Medium new potatoes   3 to 4, parboiled until nearly tender
Unsalted butter   ½ cup
Celery   ½ cup chopped
Onion   ¾ cup chopped
Mushrooms   ¾ cup sliced
Flour   ¼ cup
Chicken broth   2½ to 3 cups
Artichoke hearts   two 8½-ounce cans, quartered, juice reserved
Red pepper   ¼ teaspoon ground
Fresh thyme   ¾ teaspoon or
    Dried thyme   ¼ teaspoon
Fresh oregano   ¾ teaspoon or
    Dried oregano   ¼ teaspoon
Sage   ¼ teaspoon
Cream   1 cup
Salt and pepper   to taste

1. Slice new potatoes after parboiling. Set aside.
2. Melt 2 tablespoons butter in large, heavy skillet over medium heat. Add celery, onion, and mushrooms and sauté until vegetables are soft and onion is translucent, 10 to 15 minutes. Set aside.
3. Melt remaining butter in large pot over low heat. Add flour and cook, stirring constantly, 5 minutes. Stir in vegetables. Add broth slowly, stirring constantly. Add artichoke hearts with juice and seasonings and stir through. Increase heat to medium and simmer 30 minutes, stirring occasionally.
4. Beat cream in small bowl just until frothy. Blend into soup. Heat through; do not boil. Adjust seasoning. Serve immediately.

Potato and Seafood Bisque
Serves 4

An impressive first course or luncheon soup featuring shrimp or crab.

Medium onion 1, chopped
Celery ½ cup chopped
Butter 2 tablespoons
Medium waxy potatoes 2, cubed
Parsley 2 tablespoons chopped
Mushrooms ½ cup sliced
Chicken broth 2 cups
Milk 2 cups
Shrimp or crab meat ¼ to ½ pound
Cornstarch 1½ tablespoons
Water 3 tablespoons
Salt and pepper to taste
Butter to taste
Parsley garnish

1. In a 3-quart pan over medium heat, cook onion and celery in 2 tablespoons butter until onion is limp.
2. Add potatoes, parsley, mushrooms, and broth. Bring to a boil; cover, reduce heat, and simmer until potatoes are tender.
3. Stir in milk and seafood and cook, covered, until soup is thoroughly hot, but not boiling.
4. Place cornstarch in small cup and add water gradually, stirring until it forms paste. Add to soup and cook until soup bubbles and thickens slightly (about 5 minutes). Season to taste with salt and pepper. Serve hot, garnishing each serving with a small pat of butter and chopped parsley.

Cream of Vegetable Soup Normandy
Serves 6 to 8

Winter vegetables blended in creamy perfection make this a savory and nourishing soup. Use as a first course or as a mealtime mainstay with crusty bread, a lively salad, fresh fruit with cheese, and your favorite wine.

Butter ¼ cup
Medium carrots 5 to 6, thinly sliced
Medium leeks 3, sliced (white parts with some green)
Medium onions 2, thinly sliced
Medium turnips 2, peeled and thinly sliced
Medium potatoes 6, sliced
Chicken stock 8 cups
Salt and pepper to taste
Crème Fraîche

1. Melt butter in dutch oven or large saucepan over medium heat. Add carrots, leeks, onions, and turnips and sauté until golden.
2. Add potatoes, stock, and salt and pepper to taste. Increase heat and bring to boil. Reduce heat and simmer until vegetables are very tender. Transfer to blender or processor in small batches and puree. Return to pan and stir in Crème Fraîche. Cook over low heat until just warmed through (do not boil). Serve immediately.

Crème Fraîche
Makes 1 cup

Whipping cream 1 cup
Buttermilk 1 tablespoon

1. Combine cream and buttermilk in jar with tight-fitting lid and shake briskly 1 minute.
2. Let stand at room temperature until thickened, at least 8 hours.
3. Shake again. Refrigerate until ready to use.

Vichyssoise
Serves 4

Nothing could be more refreshing on a hot summer's day than a velvety smooth, ice-cold bowl of vichyssoise. Served hot, it makes a fine first course.

Medium leeks   3, sliced (white part only)
Medium onion   1, quartered and sliced
Butter   2 tablespoons
Medium potatoes   4, peeled and thinly sliced
Chicken stock   4 cups
Salt and pepper   to taste
Cream   1 to 2 cups
Chives   garnish

1. Sauté leeks and onion in butter until onion turns yellow (about 3 minutes).
2. Add potatoes and stock and simmer vegetables, covered, until tender (about 20 minutes). Season with salt and pepper to taste.
3. Puree soup in small batches in blender, processor, or food mill. Add cream and mix well. Refrigerate several hours until thoroughly chilled or heat through, without bringing to a boil. Garnish with a sprinkling of chopped chives.

Variations: Adding fresh or frozen corn (1 to 1½ cups) along with the potatoes and stock makes a nice, slightly sweetened alternate. Or try adding 1 cup peeled, seeded, and diced cucumber when you puree the soup for an even fresher summer flavor.

Pureed Potatomato Soup
Serves 4 to 6

Potato and tomato form a winning combination in this lively, full-bodied puree. To offset the richness of the puree, serve with a beef and vegetable stir-fry and perhaps cold cooked asparagus with mustard sauce.

Vegetable oil   1½ tablespoons
Large onion   1, chopped
Green pepper   1, chopped
Fresh or canned tomatoes   2 cups peeled and chunked
Sugar   ½ teaspoon
Dried basil   1 teaspoon
Salt   1 teaspoon
Paprika   ¼ teaspoon
Potatoes   2 cups boiled, peeled, and cubed
Milk   1 cup
Butter   1 tablespoon
Potato water   2 to 3 cups
Sour cream   1 cup (optional)

1.   Heat oil in large skillet or soup kettle. Sauté onion and green pepper until golden, but not brown. Add tomatoes, sugar, basil, salt, and paprika and simmer gently until vegetables are very tender.
2.   Transfer vegetables to processor or blender and puree in small batches. Return to soup pan.
3.   Puree potatoes and milk in small batches and add to soup. Add butter.
4.   Reheat soup carefully over low heat, adding potato water until desired consistency is attained. Serve hot or cold with dollops of sour cream.

Potato-Cauliflower Puree
Serves 4

Serve this enticing soup as an elegant first course or for brunch with baked stuffed trout, steamed asparagus, and a delicate Riesling.

Large potato   1, peeled and diced
Cauliflower   1 head (about 1 pound), broken into flowerets
Cream   ½ cup
Parmesan cheese   ½ cup freshly grated
Unsalted butter   3 tablespoons
Chicken stock   2 cups
Salt and pepper   to taste
Fresh nutmeg   ½ to 1 teaspoon grated

1. Steam potato and cauliflower pieces until soft, about 12 minutes. Transfer to processor or blender.
2. Add cream, cheese, and butter. Mix until puree is completely smooth.
3. Pour ingredients into saucepan and heat over medium heat. Add stock a little at a time, stirring often. When soup reaches desired consistency and is thoroughly heated, add salt, pepper, and nutmeg to taste. Serve immediately. (Soup can be made in advance and reheated.)

Pureed Vegetable Soup
Serves 6 to 8

This exceedingly good soup owes its unique flavor to the addition of artichoke hearts.

Large potatoes 2, diced
Medium leeks 3, white parts only, chopped
Medium carrots 3, sliced
Green beans 1 cup cut
Parsley several sprigs
Garlic cloves 2, minced
Salt 2 teaspoons
Chicken broth 1 quart
Water 1 quart
Frozen artichoke hearts 10-ounce package, cooked
Pimiento ½ cup diced
Salt and pepper to taste
Cream ½ cup
Butter 3 tablespoons

1. In large soup kettle, combine potatoes, leeks, carrots, green beans, parsley, garlic, and 2 teaspoons salt in chicken broth and water and simmer about 40 minutes. Vegetables should be very tender.
2. Add precooked artichoke hearts and pimiento (reserving several of each for garnish). Simmer for an additional 10 minutes so flavors combine.
3. Puree soup in small batches in blender or food processor, then return to kettle.
4. Add salt and pepper to taste. Add cream and butter. Slowly reheat, stirring occasionally until butter melts and soup is well blended. Taste and season as desired.
5. Chop reserved artichoke hearts and pimiento and sprinkle a small amount on each serving.

Pureed Potato and Parsnip Soup
Serves 4

This is a subtly sweet, creamy soup that makes an excellent first course, especially during winter months when parsnips are sweeter and have a more delicate taste. Select small to medium parsnips to avoid woody centers.

Potatoes   2, chunked
Salt   ½ teaspoon
Parsnips   2, chunked
Butter   3 tablespoons
Cream or half-and-half   1½ cups
Salt and pepper   to taste
Chives or green onions   garnish

1. Cover potatoes with cold water. Add ¼ teaspoon salt and cook for 15 to 20 minutes, until tender.
2. Cover parsnips with cold water, add ¼ teaspoon salt, and bring to a gentle boil. Cook parsnips 8 to 10 minutes, until very tender.
3. Remove parsnips and potatoes from cooking liquid (reserve liquid) and puree each with 1 tablespoon butter. Combine in soup pan.
4. Add remaining 1 tablespoon butter and heat pureed vegetables until butter is melted. Add cream and enough of reserved cooking liquid to give soup desired consistency. (Use parsnip water first, potato as needed.)
5. Heat soup over low heat until uniformly warm. Season with salt and pepper to taste, garnish with chives, and serve.

Oyster Stew
Serves 4 to 6

Oyster lovers will find it hard to resist this basic, but rich version of oyster stew. Served with oyster crackers and crisp coleslaw, it's a traditional American favorite.

Potatoes   2, diced
Water   1 cup
Salt   1 to 2 teaspoons
Oysters   1 pint, drained and chopped (reserve liquor)
Oyster liquor   2 cups (add milk, if necessary, to make 2 cups)
Butter   ¼ to ½ cup
Cream   1 cup
Pepper   to taste
Paprika   ¼ teaspoon

1. Cook potatoes in water with 1 teaspoon salt until almost soft, about 10 minutes.
2. Add chopped oysters and liquor and bring just to a boil. Remove from heat immediately to avoid overcooking oysters.
3. Add butter, cream, and seasonings to taste. Stir and return to heat, carefully reheating to serving temperature. Serve at once.

Shaker Winter Stew
Serves 6

This thick, robust Shaker stew has a rich flavor and a creamy consistency. Crisped pieces of salt pork are a nice contrast to the slightly sweet taste of the parsnips.

Salt pork 2- or 3-inch cube, diced
Large onion 1, diced
Medium potatoes 2, diced
Parsnips 2, diced
Chicken stock or water 2 to 3 cups
Butter 2 tablespoons
Flour 2 tablespoons
Milk 1 cup
Cream 1 cup, room temperature
Salt and pepper to taste

1. Sauté salt pork slowly in a heavy soup kettle. Remove pieces with slotted spoon when crisp and golden.
2. Sauté onion in pork fat until color turns. Add potatoes, parsnips, and stock. Cover and simmer until vegetables are tender.
3. Melt butter, add flour, and whisk together until mixture bubbles. Add milk slowly, stirring until white sauce thickens.
4. Pour sauce into soup and mix well. Bring to boil, remove from heat, and add cream. Season to taste. Sprinkle with salt pork pieces and serve.

Hunters' Stew
Serves 4

A delicious, rib-sticking stew that is sure to send your hunters out feeling satisfied and well nourished.

Salad oil   2 tablespoons
Boneless pork shoulder   1 pound, cut into 1-inch cubes
Medium onion   1, chopped
Garlic clove   1, minced
Mushrooms   1¼ cups sliced
Sage   ½ teaspoon crumbled
Rosemary   ¼ teaspoon crumbled
Flour   2 tablespoons
Chicken stock   3 to 4 cups
Medium potato   1, boiled and peeled
Polish sausage (kielbasa)   ¾ pound, cut into ½-inch slices
Medium potatoes   2, diced
Medium carrots   3, sliced
Wine or cider vinegar   1 tablespoon
Salt and pepper   to taste
Frozen peas   10-ounce package (optional)

1. Heat oil in large stew pot or dutch oven. Add pork, onion, garlic, mushrooms, sage, and rosemary. Sauté, stirring occasionally, until meat is lightly browned.
2. Sprinkle flour over meat mixture and stir until no dry flour is visible. Add chicken broth, stir well, and bring to a boil. Reduce heat and simmer 1 hour.
3. Rice or mash boiled potato. Add to pot and mix well.
4. Add sausage, potatoes, and carrots and stir to combine. Cover pot and continue simmering until vegetables are tender, stirring occasionally.
5. Add vinegar. Season to taste with salt and pepper. (In another pan, cook peas until tender, following directions on package. Stir peas into cooked stew.)

Iranian Green Vegetable and Meat Stew
Serves 4

Tangy and somewhat spicy, this makes an unusual and healthful meal-in-one.

Boneless stewing beef or lamb   ¾ to 1 pound
Medium onion   1, finely chopped
Vegetable oil or ghee*   3 tablespoons
Turmeric   ½ teaspoon
Water   ¾ to 1 cup
Lemon juice   2 to 3 tablespoons
Salt and pepper   to taste
Medium potatoes   2, diced
Green onions   ½ cup chopped
Spinach   1½ to 2 cups chopped
Parsley   ½ cup chopped
Fresh cilantro   ½ cup chopped (optional)

1. Trim meat and cut into ¾-inch cubes.
2. In a heavy pan gently fry onion in 1½ tablespoons oil until transparent. Add turmeric and fry for 2 additional minutes.
3. Increase heat, add meat, and sauté over high heat until meat begins to brown. Reduce heat.
4. Add water, lemon juice, and salt and pepper to taste. Cover and simmer gently for 1 to 1½ hours until meat is just tender.
5. Heat remaining oil in large frying pan and add potatoes. Fry over high heat until lightly browned. Add to meat, leaving fat in pan. Cover and simmer 10 minutes.
6. Add greens to frying pan and sauté until wilted. Add to stew, cover, and simmer an additional 15 to 20 minutes or until meat and potatoes are tender. Adjust seasoning and serve.
* Ghee can be purchased at Middle Eastern or food specialty stores.

Savory Beef and Vegetable Stew
Serves 4 to 5

Slow cooked and subtly seasoned, few foods can rival this delicious stew.

Bacon strips   5, cut into 1-inch pieces
Boneless beef chuck   2 pounds, cut into 2-inch chunks
Salt and pepper   to taste
Small white onions   4 to 6, peeled
Flour   2 tablespoons
Dry red wine   1 to 1½ cups
Beef broth   1 cup
Garlic cloves   2, minced
Orange peel   1 strip, 1 inch by 4 inches
Marjoram   ½ teaspoon
Thyme   ½ teaspoon
Medium onion   1, studded with
     Whole cloves   4
Butter   2 tablespoons
Small mushrooms   ¼ to ½ pound whole
Medium carrots   2 to 3, cut into ½-inch slices
Medium new potatoes   3 to 4, quartered
Parsley   3 tablespoons chopped (optional)

1. Preheat oven to 325°.
2. In a wide frying pan over medium heat, cook bacon until browned and crumbly. Remove with slotted spoon and place in a deep, 3-quart casserole; reserve drippings.
3. Sprinkle beef with salt and pepper; add to bacon drippings and cook, turning to brown on all sides. Remove from pan and place in casserole.
4. To pan juices, add white onions. Cook, shaking pan occasionally, until lightly browned. Remove from pan; reserve juices.
5. Stir flour into pan juices and cook until bubbly. Gradually pour in wine and broth and continue cooking, stirring often until sauce thickens. Add garlic, orange peel, marjoram, and thyme. Mix, then pour over beef in casserole. Tuck clove-studded onion down into liquid.
6. Bake, covered, for 2½ hours.
7. Meanwhile, in same frying pan, melt butter over medium heat. Add mushrooms, carrots, and potatoes and cook until juices have evaporated; set aside.
8. When stew has baked for 2½ hours, add browned onions, mushrooms, carrots, and potatoes. Push them down into liquid, cover, and return to oven for about 30 more minutes or until vegetables are tender. Remove studded onion and sprinkle with parsley, if desired.

Clam Chowder
Serves 4 to 8

There is nothing exotic about this chowder—it is simply good. Of course, you can jazz it up if you like by adding crab or shrimp or mushrooms. But we prefer a "generic" chowder, which does not obscure the flavor of fresh clams and potatoes.

Bacon strips   6, diced
Large onion   ½, chopped
Garlic clove   1, minced
Celery stalks   3, chopped
Large russet potatoes   3, diced
Water   4 to 5 cups
Clam nectar   1 cup (reserved from steamed clams or bottled)
Salt and pepper   to taste
Fresh clams   2½ pounds, steamed or
   Canned clams   two 6½-ounce cans
Cream or half-and-half   ½ to 1 cup

1. Sauté bacon in heavy saucepan over moderate heat. Add onion, garlic, and celery and sauté until limp.
2. Add potatoes, water, and clam nectar. Salt and pepper to taste. Cook over medium-high heat for 30 minutes to 1 hour, maintaining a low boil. (Gauge your cooking time according to how mushy you prefer your chowder.)
3. Remove pan from heat and stir in clams and cream. Return to heat only long enough to warm cream thoroughly.

Potato, Corn, and Shrimp Chowder
Serves 4

This is a slight modification of an old favorite from The Pooh Cook Book *by Virginia H. Ellison. Putting it together is virtually child's play, and the result is a satisfying supper—or "smackeral" or "little something" as Pooh might say.*

Medium onion   1, diced
Butter or margarine   1 tablespoon
Clam nectar   1 cup (fresh or bottled)
Large potato   1, boiled and diced
Cream-style corn   17-ounce can
Thyme   ¼ teaspoon
Fresh or frozen shrimp*   1 cup
Cream or milk   1 cup
Salt and pepper   to taste
Paprika   dash
Parsley   garnish

1. Lightly brown onion in butter in a heavy-bottomed pot, 2-quart size or larger. Add clam nectar, potato, corn, and thyme and set over low heat. Let simmer for 5 minutes.
2. Add shrimp and simmer until shrimp are pink and tender (or other fish is cooked through). Add cream and heat again, this time just to boiling point.
3. Add salt and pepper to taste. Dust with paprika and garnish with chopped parsley. Serve in hot soup bowls.

* Any kind of fish may be substituted for shrimp, such as tuna, cod, or halibut.

Corn Chowder
Serves 4 to 6

A luscious, gratifying soup, this is the distillation of several corn chowders.

Salt pork   ¼ cup diced
Butter   1 tablespoon
Medium onion   1, chopped
Celery stalk   1, chopped
Green pepper   ½, seeded and chopped
Medium potatoes   3, peeled and diced
Chicken stock   2 cups
Fresh corn scraped from the cob   1½ to 2 cups or
      Canned cream-style corn   17-ounce can
Pimiento   2 tablespoons chopped
Milk   2 cups
Flour   2 tablespoons
Paprika   ¼ to ½ teaspoon
Salt and pepper   to taste
Cream   ½ cup
Butter   2 tablespoons (optional)

1. Slowly fry salt pork in butter until crispy. Remove with slotted spoon, drain, and reserve. Add onions to fat and sauté until golden.
2. Add celery, green pepper, potatoes, and stock and simmer until tender.
3. Add corn, pimiento, and milk. Simmer about 5 minutes longer (until corn is tender).
4. Remove about ½ cup hot broth and mix with flour until blended. Return mixture to soup, stirring well. Heat through until soup thickens slightly. Season with paprika, salt, and pepper.
5. Bring soup to a boil, remove from heat, and stir in cream and butter. Serve with pork cubes sprinkled on top.

Potato and Broccoli Chowder
Serves 4 to 6

A perfect use for that last piece of leftover ham, this chowder is quickly prepared and nutritious enough to be a meal mainstay.

Potatoes   2 cups diced
Chicken stock   2 cups
Broccoli   1 pound, coarsely chopped
Cooked ham   1 cup chopped
Milk   2 cups
Half-and-half or cream   ½ cup
Swiss cheese   1 cup grated
Butter   ¼ cup
Salt and pepper   to taste

1. ▪ Combine potatoes and chicken stock in kettle and simmer for 10 minutes. Add broccoli and continue cooking until broccoli is just tender, about 7 minutes.
2. Add remaining ingredients, bring to just below boiling point, reduce heat to low, and simmer about 10 more minutes. Serve at once.

Side
Dishes

Potato Knishes
Serves 8 to 10

Knishes are one of many "pocket" foods originating in Eastern Europe. They can be filled with innumerable combinations; potatoes and onions are among the most popular.

Flour   1¾ cups
Gluten flour*   ¼ cup
Vegetable shortening   6 tablespoons
Salt   ¼ teaspoon
Cold water   4 to 5 tablespoons
Medium baking potatoes   6, peeled and cubed
Vegetable oil   ½ cup
Salt   ½ teaspoon
Pepper   ⅛ teaspoon
Large yellow onions   3, thinly sliced
Egg yolk   1

1. In food processor or by hand, combine flours, add shortening, and blend.
2. Dissolve salt in water and add to processor while running until dough forms a ball, or mix by hand until dough forms a ball. Let dough rest in refrigerator while preparing filling.
3. Cook potatoes in salted boiling water until tender but not mushy. Drain. Set aside.
4. Place oil and seasonings in large pan and cook (do not fry) the onions over moderate heat until they are very soft, about 20 to 25 minutes.
5. Rice or mash potatoes, add onions, and the oil in which onions were cooked. Mix well and correct seasonings.
6. Preheat oven to 500°. Roll out dough on a lightly floured surface to ⅛-inch thickness. The sheet of dough should be approximately 2 feet square.
7. Using half of potato mixture, form a long, straight mound of filling over dough ½ inch in from the edges. Gently pat the mound to flatten it.
8. Bring up edge of dough to partially cover filling and continue rolling dough until filling is completely covered. Using a sharp knife, cut filled roll away from remaining dough.
9. Cut roll at 2¼-inch intervals. Place knishes on a well-greased cookie sheet, sides touching. (Don't pinch the sides closed.) Brush with beaten

egg yolk. Bake for 15 minutes and remove from oven as soon as they become golden brown. Repeat with remaining dough and filling. The knishes may be frozen and then reheated at 350° for about 25 minutes before serving.

* Gluten flour is available at health food stores. It makes the dough extra crispy.

Gnocchi Florentine
Serves 6

These rich and hearty Italian "dumplings" have been a universal hit with our tasting audience. Serve them with something light like a spinach soufflé and you will strike exactly the right balance.

Water or milk 1 cup
Butter ⅓ cup
Flour 1 cup
Salt ⅛ teaspoon
Eggs 4 to 5, room temperature
Mashed potatoes 2 cups
Parmesan cheese ½ cup
Ham 1 cup finely chopped
Oregano ¼ teaspoon
Parmesan cheese 3 tablespoons grated
Butter 2 tablespoons melted

1. Preheat oven to 400°.
2. Bring water and ⅓ cup butter to boil in heavy pan. Add flour and salt and stir hard until smooth and dough leaves the sides of pan. Remove from heat and beat in eggs singly.
3. Add potatoes, ½ cup cheese, ham, and oregano to flour mixture.
4. Shape mixture into balls about 1 tablespoon each. Nest together in buttered, shallow baking dish. Sprinkle 3 tablespoons cheese and dribble 2 tablespoons butter over top of gnocchi.
5. Bake for 25 minutes.

Pommes Duchesse
Serves 4

Mashed potatoes take on an elegant air when used in this classic recipe.

Mashed potatoes 2 cups
Egg yolks 2
Butter 2 tablespoons
Cream 2 tablespoons
Salt and pepper to taste
Parmesan cheese garnish
Paprika garnish

1. Combine mashed potatoes, egg yolks, butter, and cream. Beat until smooth. Add salt and pepper to taste.
2. Arrange spoonfuls of mixture on greased cookie sheet or on oven-proof plates, or pipe through a pastry bag fitted with a decorative tip and use around the border of serving plates.
3. Just before serving, preheat broiler. Dust potatoes with parmesan and paprika. Broil until golden and serve.

Potatoes Gratin
Serves 4 to 5

This is one of the simplest, most reliable, and most delicious gratins we've tried. Of course, you can add sausage, ham, or any other kind of leftover meats to make this an entrée, but it is excellent by itself.

New potatoes 4 to 5 cups thinly sliced
Salt and pepper to taste
Whipping cream 1 to 1½ cups
Gruyère cheese ¾ to 1 cup shredded

1. Preheat oven to 325°.
2. Place potato slices in shallow 1½-quart casserole. Level potatoes, sprinkle lightly with salt and pepper, and pour in cream to barely cover potatoes.
3. Bake, uncovered, for 1 hour. Remove casserole from oven, sprinkle shredded cheese over potatoes, and bake about 20 minutes longer or until golden.

Cabbage, Potatoes, and Apples au Gratin
Serves 4 to 6

Serve this pleasing Irish classic with corned beef and Irish soda bread for your own St. Patrick's Day feast.

Small green cabbage   1, thinly sliced
Large baking potatoes   2, thinly sliced
Apples   2 to 3, peeled, cored, and thinly sliced
Medium onion   1, finely chopped
Salt and pepper   to taste
Butter   3 to 4 tablespoons
Cream   1 cup
Fine bread crumbs   ¼ cup
Swiss cheese   ¼ cup grated

1. Preheat oven to 350°.
2. Arrange a third of cabbage, potatoes, apples, and onion in a large, buttered casserole. Season with salt and pepper and dot with butter. Continue layering, piling vegetables high in the center of casserole (the dish will be quite full, but the vegetables will cook down).
3. Pour in cream and cover casserole. Bake for 45 minutes or until just tender.
4. Sprinkle bread crumbs and cheese over top and return casserole to oven, uncovered, for 20 minutes or until top is browned and crusty.

Colcannon
Serves 4

Colcannon is another classic Irish dish. Traditionally served on Halloween (as well as throughout the year), the cook might place some charms in the colcannon for lucky diners to find in their helpings.

Green onions   3 to 4
Milk   ⅓ cup
Mashed potatoes   2 cups
Cooked cabbage   2 cups chopped or shredded
Salt and pepper   to taste
Butter   4 tablespoons

1. Preheat oven to 350°.
2. Finely chop green onions using both the white and some green parts. Put them in a saucepan with the milk and bring to just below the boiling point; set aside.
3. Combine potatoes and cabbage in a mixing bowl. Season with salt and pepper. Pour in milk and green onions and mix well. Transfer to a greased casserole and bake for 20 minutes.
4. Make several holes in top of colcannon and put a pat of butter in each hole. Serve immediately.

Heavenly Potatoes
Serves 8

Potato "cloud" would be another apt name for these deluxe mashed potatoes. They are too rich for everyday fare, but will add the perfect touch to a Sunday fried chicken dinner.

Medium potatoes   6
Salt   1 teaspoon
Pepper   ¼ teaspoon
Butter   ½ cup
Milk   ⅓ cup (more or less as needed)
Cheddar cheese   1 cup grated
Whipping cream   1 cup, whipped

1. Preheat oven to 350°
2. Boil potatoes in jackets in salted water until tender. Drain, skin, and mash. Add seasonings, butter, and milk, then beat until fluffy and creamy. Taste and adjust seasonings.
3. Place potatoes in greased 2-quart casserole.
4. Fold cheese into whipped cream and spread over potatoes. Bake until golden brown, 20 to 25 minutes.

Swiss Country Mashed Potatoes with Pears
Serves 4

This is a traditional dish in rural, German-speaking Switzerland. It is a slightly sweet side dish that is very popular with children and that is especially good with pork dishes.

Pear or apple 1, cored and sliced
Water ¼ cup
White wine ¼ cup
Sugar ¼ cup
Cinnamon ½ teaspoon
Whole clove 1
Lemon rind ¼ teaspoon grated
Mashed potatoes 2 cups
Soft bread crumbs ¾ cup
Butter 2 tablespoons

1. Preheat oven to 350°.
2. In a small saucepan place first 7 ingredients and bring to a boil. Reduce heat and simmer until pears are quite tender. Discard clove.
3. Butter a 2-quart casserole dish and arrange in it a layer of mashed potatoes, then a layer of sliced pears with sauce. Repeat layering, ending with mashed potatoes and remainder of sauce.
4. Either brown bread crumbs in butter and spoon over mixture or add bread crumbs and dabs of butter to casserole and switch oven to broil at end of baking time, just long enough to brown.
5. Bake for about 15 minutes and serve.

Potato Soufflé with Cheese and Olives
Serves 6

This is a moist, heavy soufflé with a savory combination of flavors.

Hot mashed potatoes 2 cups
Butter 3 tablespoons
Sour cream 1 cup
Sharp cheddar cheese 1 cup grated
Egg yolks 4
Salt and pepper to taste
Black olives ½ cup chopped, well-drained
Chives or green onions 4 tablespoons chopped
Egg whites 4
Salt pinch
Cream of tartar pinch

1. Preheat oven to 350°.
2. Combine mashed potatoes, butter, sour cream, cheese, egg yolks, and salt and pepper in a large mixing bowl. Blend well. (This is easily done in blender or processor.) Stir in chopped olives and chives.
3. Beat egg whites with pinch of salt and cream of tartar until stiff. Carefully fold into potato mixture and pile into oiled 2-quart casserole.
4. Bake for 45 to 50 minutes, until top is golden and toothpick inserted in center comes out dry. Serve at once.

Note: The following are several hints that will help you make a perfect soufflé:

(1) When you butter a casserole dish for the soufflé, dust it with parmesan cheese; tap and tilt until dish has an even coating. This makes a great crust.

(2) When mixing the egg whites by hand or with a mixer, try to get as much volume as possible. Beat until stiff, but not dry. (An additional egg white for every 2 eggs will make a soufflé even lighter.)

(3) To fold in egg whites, add about a third of egg whites to mixture first. This will lighten mixture so that the remaining egg whites will blend more easily without loss of volume.

(4) Waste no time between beating egg whites, folding them in, and popping soufflé into preheated oven. Place in center of oven with plenty of room for expansion on top.

Potato and Onion Soufflé
Serves 6

A slightly spicy, feathery soufflé with satisfying bites of potato and onion.

Butter   5 tablespoons
Flour   3 tablespoons
Milk   1⅓ cups, scalded
Egg yolks   6, room temperature
Jack or other mild cheese   1 cup grated
Dijon mustard   1 to 2 teaspoons
Tabasco sauce   ½ to 1 teaspoon (optional)
Medium potato   1 (about ½ pound), diced
Medium yellow onion   1, quartered and thinly sliced
Salt   1 teaspoon
Egg whites   8, beaten
Cream of tartar   pinch
Parmesan cheese   pinch

1. Preheat oven to 375°.
2. Melt 3 tablespoons butter in large saucepan, stir in flour, and cook several minutes over low heat, stirring constantly. Add hot milk and whisk until sauce thickens and is smooth. Remove pan from heat and beat in egg yolks, 1 at a time. Stir in cheese, mustard, and tabasco and return to low heat until cheese melts. Set aside.
3. Peel potato, cut into small dice, and boil in salted water until just tender. Drain. Slice onion. Melt 2 tablespoons butter in medium skillet. Add onions and sauté until they begin to color. Then add potato. Continue cooking, turning often, until potatoes are golden. Add potatoes and onion to cheese sauce, salt, and mix.
4. Beat egg whites with cream of tartar until stiff. Carefully fold into cheese and vegetable mixture, then pour into generously buttered 2-quart casserole that has been sprinkled with parmesan cheese. (See Index for general information on preparing successful soufflés.)
5. Place casserole in preheated oven. Lower heat immediately to 350° and bake for about 45 minutes, until golden and firm. Serve at once.

Mashed Potato Casserole
Serves 4

Creamy, cheesy, and golden brown, this casserole makes a great accompaniment to roast turkey, chicken, or beef.

Cream cheese   3-ounce package, softened
Garlic clove   1, minced
Salt   ¼ teaspoon
Pepper   to taste
Sour cream   ½ cup
Medium baking potatoes   3 to 4, peeled and cooked
Butter   2 tablespoons
Paprika   garnish

1. Preheat oven to 400°.
2. In a bowl, stir together cream cheese, garlic, salt, pepper, and sour cream until smooth; set aside.
3. Using an electric mixer or a potato masher, beat hot potatoes until they are in fine lumps.
4. Add cream cheese mixture and continue beating until fluffy and smooth. Spoon potatoes into a well-buttered, shallow, 2-quart casserole; dot with butter and sprinkle with paprika. (If made ahead, cover and refrigerate until next day.)
5. Bake, covered, for 25 minutes (50 minutes, if refrigerated); uncover and bake for 10 more minutes or until top is golden brown.

Potato and Spinach Gratin with Anchovy Butter
Serves 4

This mild and flavorful casserole takes on new zest with the addition of an-chovy butter. Serve with steaks, roasted meat, or broiled fish such as fresh tuna or sardines.

Spinach   3 cups chopped
Chicken stock   ½ cup
Swiss cheese   ¾ to 1 cup grated
Medium boiling potatoes   2 to 3, boiled and cut into thin slices
Anchovy Butter
Bread crumbs   ½ cup
Butter   2 tablespoons melted

1. Preheat oven to 375°.
2. Braise spinach in stock until just tender. Add ½ cup cheese and set aside.
3. Spread half of potatoes on bottom of a lightly buttered 9-inch square casserole. Cover with half of Anchovy Butter, then half of spinach mixture. Repeat layering.
4. Mix remaining cheese with bread crumbs and spread over top. Pour melted butter over casserole and bake for 30 minutes or until top is nicely browned.

Anchovy Butter
Makes 5 to 6 tablespoons

Whole anchovies   2 tablespoons mashed or
   Anchovy paste   1 tablespoon
Butter   4 tablespoons, softened
Pepper   ⅛ teaspoon

1. Blend all ingredients thoroughly.

Gratin aux Champignons
Serves 4

If you are a mushroom fan, you will love this casserole, for the flavor of the mushroom juice permeates each bite. And if you are lucky or enterprising enough to have some wild mushrooms on hand like boletes or morels, you might want to mix a few with their tamer, domestic cousins.

Garlic clove   1, peeled
Butter   ½ cup
Medium potatoes   4 to 5, thinly sliced
Salt and pepper   to taste
Mushrooms   1 to 1½ pounds, sliced
Swiss cheese   1½ to 2 cups grated
Parsley   1 clump, chopped
Small onion   1, minced
Cream   1 to 1½ cups

1. Preheat oven to 375°.
2. Rub a 2-quart baking dish with garlic clove and butter it well with 2 to 3 tablespoons butter.
3. Arrange some potato slices in bottom; salt and pepper to taste. Follow with a layer of mushrooms, some grated cheese, parsley, and onion. Continue layering, ending with potatoes.
4. Pour cream over mixture. Add a sprinkling of cheese and dot with remaining butter.
5. Bake for 1 hour or until potatoes are tender and top is bubbly and browned.

Potatoes Gruyère
Serves 4 to 6

This is one of the best scalloped potato and cheese dishes we've tasted.

Sour cream   1 cup
Gruyère cheese   1 cup grated
Small onion   1, finely chopped
Chives or green onions   2 tablespoons chopped
Butter   2 tablespoons
Medium potatoes   4 to 5, thinly sliced
Salt and pepper   to taste
Bread crumbs   ½ cup
Parmesan cheese   ¼ cup grated (optional)

1. Preheat oven to 350°.
2. Mix together sour cream, gruyère, onion, and chives.
3. Butter a 2½-quart casserole with 1 tablespoon butter and arrange a layer of potatoes on bottom of dish; salt and pepper well. Follow this with a layer of half the sour cream mixture, and so on, finishing with the rest of sour cream mixture on top.
4. Sprinkle top with bread crumbs and parmesan, dot with remaining 1 tablespoon butter, and cover. Bake for 1½ hours. Remove lid and bake additional 15 to 20 minutes. Serve steaming hot.

Potato and Corn Scallop

Serves 4 to 6

Buttermilk gives this dish a pleasing hint of tartness. As with most scallop dishes, it is easily assembled in advance and requires little further attention. Serve as a side dish or as a main brunch or supper dish with an accompanying green salad.

Baking potatoes 4 to 5, thinly sliced
Salt and pepper to taste
Fresh corn 2 cups scraped from ears or
    Frozen corn 10-ounce package
Jack cheese 1½ cups grated
Green onions or chives 3 tablespoons chopped
Butter 4 tablespoons
Buttermilk 2 cups

1. Preheat oven to 375°.
2. Place half of potato slices in a single layer on bottom of buttered, 2-quart casserole. Season with salt and pepper. Sprinkle with half of corn and cheese and 1 tablespoon green onions. Dot with half of butter. Repeat layering, ending with thin layer of potatoes. Pour buttermilk over.
3. Bake for 1 to 1¼ hours until buttermilk is absorbed and potatoes are tender with crusty, brown top. Sprinkle with remaining green onion and serve.

Scalloped Potatoes and Carrots with Cream
Serves 4 to 6

A delicious, rich casserole laced with sweet braised carrots. Makes a mouth-watering companion to any roast meats.

Carrots   2 cups cut into ⅛-inch slices
Butter   ½ tablespoon
Salt   ¼ teaspoon
Shallots or green onions   2 tablespoons finely minced
Water   ¾ cup
Butter   4 tablespoons
Medium boiling potatoes   4 to 5, cut into ⅛-inch slices
Salt and pepper   to taste
Swiss cheese   1 cup grated
Cream   1¼ cups

1. Preheat oven to 300°.
2. Boil carrots slowly with ½ tablespoon butter, salt, shallots, and water in a covered saucepan for about 15 minutes, or until carrots are tender.
3. Butter a 2½-quart casserole dish with 1 tablespoon butter. Arrange a layer of potato slices in it, followed by a layer of braised carrots. Sprinkle with salt, pepper, cheese, and dots of butter. Repeat layering, ending with cheese and butter.
4. Pour cream over top and heat the casserole on top of stove until it is almost simmering. Place in the middle of oven and bake slowly for 1 to 1¼ hours. Check temperature occasionally to be sure cream does not boil (to prevent curdling). The gratin is done when potatoes are tender, the cream is absorbed, and the top is lightly browned.

Mrs. Goldschmid's Potato "Scarabs"
Serves 4

This recipe was given to us by a dear friend, Nicoletta Misch, with the following note: "Forgive me, dear Mrs. Goldschmid, wherever you are now, for breaking the promise of keeping this recipe to myself. It was given to me as thanks for a favor, long forgotten, and so many hungry hearts have been pacified with your recipe that I like to think you agree that it should be divulged to posterity. . . . The name 'Scarabs' was given to the dish by Mrs. Pellegrini, who exclaimed this word when she saw the baking sheet full of brown . . . well, scarabs!"

Baking potatoes 4 (of similar size for easier timing)
Salt 1 teaspoon
Caraway seeds 1 teaspoon
Butter 4 to 8 tablespoons

1. Preheat oven to 400°.
2. Scrub potatoes and cut in half lengthwise.
3. Make a mound for each potato of ¼ teaspoon each salt and caraway seeds on cutting board. Press moist, cut side of potatoes onto mounds.
4. Place potatoes, cut side down, on buttered cookie sheet.
5. Make 1 lengthwise gash about ½ inch deep along back of each potato. Then score with 2 or 3 crosswise slits. Dot with butter.
6. Bake for 40 to 60 minutes, until potatoes are tender and undersides have developed a crisp, brown crust.

Potato Brioches
Serves 3 to 4

This is a fun and flavorful side dish—mashed potato "muffins" or rolls, with crunchy tops and centers full of oozing melted cheese.

Medium potatoes   3, peeled and cut into chunks
Butter   2 tablespoons
Salt and pepper   to taste
Nutmeg   pinch
Egg yolk   1
Swiss, cheddar, or mozzarella cheese   six to eight 1-inch cubes
Egg   1, lightly beaten
Fine bread crumbs   2 to 3 tablespoons
Parmesan cheese   2 tablespoons grated (optional)

1. Preheat oven to 400°.
2. Boil potatoes in salted water until tender. Drain, mash, or put through ricer. Add butter, salt, pepper, and nutmeg to potatoes and mix well. Add egg yolk, stir, and blend.
3. Generously grease 6 to 8 muffin tins or small molds. Fill each three-quarters full with potato mixture.
4. Press a cheese cube into center of each brioche. Brush tops with beaten egg, sprinkle with bread crumbs and parmesan (if desired), and bake for about 25 minutes. Unmold and serve immediately.

Baked Potatoes à la Grecque
Serves 6

This is a very simple, but very good version of a baked potato. The lemon juice gives it a flavor that goes well with any seafood dish or with something like charbroiled lamb kabobs.

Large baking potatoes   6
Butter   4 to 6 tablespoons, softened
Salt and pepper   to taste
Lemon juice   from 1 lemon

1. Preheat oven to 350°.
2. Halve potatoes lengthwise and spread each half generously with butter. Sprinkle the halves with salt, pepper, and lemon juice.
3. Bake potato halves on cookie sheet for about 45 minutes or until tender when pierced with a fork.

Baked Potato "Chips"

A strikingly simple departure from traditional baked potatoes, these "chips" are crispy and slightly puffed.

Baking potato   1 per person
Olive or vegetable oil   1 teaspoon (to oil cookie sheet)
Butter   1 to 2 tablespoons per person

1. Preheat oven to 450°.
2. Cut potatoes into eighths or smaller.
3. Lay potato pieces out on oiled cookie sheet and dot with butter. Bake until puffy and crisp, turning occasionally to prevent sticking. (About 40 minutes, until golden.)

Pan-Fried Baked Potatoes
Serves 4 to 5

This is a flavorful accompaniment to steaks or roasted meats, plus a good way to use leftover baked potatoes.

Butter   3 tablespoons
Olive oil   3 tablespoons
Large baking potatoes   4, baked and sliced into ¼-inch rounds
Green onions   4, chopped
Caraway seeds   ¼ to ½ teaspoon
Salt and pepper   to taste
Sour cream   1 cup

1. Heat butter and oil in large skillet. Add prebaked, sliced potatoes and sauté over medium-high heat until golden.
2. Add green onions and caraway seeds and cook just long enough for flavors to blend, turning gently.
3. Season with salt and pepper and turn out onto warmed platter. Serve with dollops of sour cream.

Roasted Potatoes with Bacon and Rosemary
Serves 8 to 10

An excellent and easy accompaniment to roast meats, these potatoes are golden and crispy outside, creamy smooth inside. The combined flavors of bacon, rosemary, olive oil, and butter are all absorbed during the long roasting and make this dish great holiday fare.

Medium new potatoes   12 to 15
Butter   ½ cup, preferably unsalted
Bacon strips*   8, blanched and chopped
Olive oil   ¼ cup
Dried rosemary   2 tablespoons or
     Fresh rosemary   8 sprigs
Salt and pepper   to taste
Fresh parsley or rosemary sprigs   garnish

1. Preheat oven to 450°.
2. Place potatoes in large pot with cold water to cover. Bring to a boil and cook for about 15 minutes. (Potatoes should still be slightly firm when pierced.) Drain, cool for several minutes, and peel.
3. In large, shallow casserole or broiler pan, melt butter, tipping to coat all surfaces. Cut potatoes into large chunks and scatter in pan. Sprinkle with bacon pieces, oil, and rosemary. Salt and pepper to taste.
4. Roast potatoes, turning often, until butter and oil are completely absorbed and potatoes are a rich golden brown. Garnish and serve in warmed, shallow serving dish.

* To blanch, place chopped bacon pieces into a pan with plenty of cold water. Slowly bring water to a boil, uncovered, and simmer a couple of minutes. Drain and plunge bacon into cold water to arrest further cooking. Drain again.

Oven-Browned Potato Wedges
Serves 4 to 6

If you like extrathick french fries, this simple recipe gives you perfectly crisp wedges with soft insides that are a great facsimile—and without the fuss of deep frying.

Medium baking potatoes   4
Butter   4 tablespoons, melted
Salt   to taste

1. Preheat oven to 450°.
2. Peel potatoes and halve lengthwise. Stand each portion upright on a chopping board and slice it in thirds down its length, making 3 wedge-shaped pieces.
3. Blanch wedges by cooking them rapidly for 3 minutes in enough un-salted boiling water to cover. Drain and pat dry with paper towels.
4. Butter a baking dish large enough to hold potatoes side by side in a single layer. Dribble melted butter over the tops and sprinkle them liberally with salt. Roast them in the center of oven for 15 minutes, turn them, and roast another 15 minutes.

Transparent Potatoes
Serves 8 to 10

This tempting side dish can complement just about any roast meat. The seasonings and beef stock are completely absorbed, creating a crusty top and bottom with creamy insides.

Beef stock   3 cups
Large garlic cloves   5 to 6
Black peppercorns   5 to 6
Medium waxy potatoes   5 to 7, peeled
Butter   ¼ cup
Fresh rosemary   2 tablespoons or
    Dried rosemary   2 teaspoons crumbled
Salt   to taste

1. Preheat oven to 375°.
2. Combine stock, garlic, and peppercorns in medium saucepan and bring to boil. Cover and simmer until garlic is tender, about 30 minutes.
3. Meanwhile, slice potatoes paper thin using vegetable peeler or thin slicer of processor and drop into cold water to prevent darkening.
4. Remove garlic and peppercorns from stock, reserving peppercorns. Sieve into stock; keep warm.
5. Melt 1 to 2 tablespoons butter in large, shallow baking dish.
6. Drain potatoes and dry thoroughly (a salad spinner works well). Add layer of potatoes to dish. Sprinkle with rosemary, salt lightly, and dot with butter. Continue layering until all potatoes are used. Pour suffi-cient stock just to cover top evenly.
7. Bake uncovered until top and bottom layers are crusty and browned, about 1¾ hours. Check after 1½ hours; if potatoes are not forming crust, increase temperature to 400°. Cut into squares and serve hot.

Potatoes Anna
Serves 6

Many potato buffs regard Potatoes Anna as the classic potato offering. Its delicately thin translucent layers and crisp, golden exterior make it a triumph of artful preparation rather than exotic ingredients.

Large russet potatoes   2 to 3
Butter   ½ cup melted
Parmesan cheese   ½ cup grated
Salt and pepper   to taste

1. Preheat oven to 425°.
2. Peel potatoes and cover with cold water. Cut potatoes into paper-thin (about ⅛-inch) slices; return slices to cold water.
3. Grease a 9-inch cake pan or a shallow 2-quart casserole. Drizzle bottom of pan with 1 tablespoon of the butter.
4. Drain potato slices on paper towels; pat dry. Arrange a sixth of the slices in an overlapping layer in pan. Drizzle potatoes with another 1 tablespoon of butter; lightly sprinkle with some cheese, salt, and pepper. Repeat layering with potatoes, butter, cheese, and seasonings; drizzle top with any remaining butter. With a heavy pan, press down potatoes to compress them.
5. Bake, covered, for about 30 minutes. Uncover and bake for 35 to 45 more minutes or until potatoes are browned and crisp on top and around edges. Let stand for 5 minutes.
6. With a large spatula, hold potatoes in place and drain off excess butter. Loosen potatoes around edges and invert on a serving platter.

Garlic Potatoes
Serves 4

For garlic lovers only! Marinated in garlic and yogurt, these perky potatoes go great with grilled meats.

Medium boiling potatoes   3, cooked until just tender
Egg   1
Yogurt   1 cup
Olive oil   ⅓ cup
Garlic cloves   2, minced
Salt   ½ teaspoon
Pepper   to taste
Yogurt   garnish (optional)

1. Slice potatoes lengthwise ½ inch thick. Arrange in shallow dish.
2. Beat egg in mixing bowl. Add remaining ingredients and blend well. Pour over sliced potatoes. Cover and refrigerate overnight.
3. Prepare barbecue or preheat broiler. Drain potatoes. Grill, turning and brushing frequently with marinade, until golden brown and fork tender, about 5 to 6 minutes. Transfer to platter. Serve with additional yogurt, if desired.

Potatoes Dauphine
Serves 4

Potatoes Dauphine are light and airy, like cream puffs, with the savory flavor of potatoes. Once cooked, they are easily stored in the refrigerator, or even frozen, and they reheat beautifully.

Medium potato 1, peeled and quartered
Egg yolk 1
Butter 1 tablespoon
Salt ½ teaspoon
Butter 3 tablespoons
Salt pinch
Water ½ cup
Flour ½ cup
Eggs 2
Oil for deep frying

1. Cook potato in water to cover until tender. Drain. Add egg yolk, 1 tablespoon butter, and ½ teaspoon salt and whip until fluffy.
2. Melt 3 tablespoons butter with salt in small saucepan. Add water and bring to boil. As soon as butter has melted, remove pan from heat and beat in flour all at once until smoothly blended. Return to heat and beat constantly until mixture leaves sides of pan and forms a mass, about 1 to 2 minutes.
3. Remove from heat and beat in eggs 1 at a time until dough is smooth and well blended. Combine flour mixture with potatoes and beat well.
4. Heat oil for deep frying to 375°. Drop mixture into oil by teaspoonfuls and cook until puffed and golden brown. Drain briefly on paper towels.
5. Serve immediately or freeze on baking sheet until firm, then pack into plastic bags or airtight containers. To reheat, bake unthawed puffs at 400° 10 to 15 minutes.

Creamed Peas and New Potatoes
Serves 4

If you have a garden and have access to those wonderful, tender quarter-sized spuds as well as fresh sweet peas, then this dish is a dream. However, you can do quite well at the farmers' market or even the corner grocery if all else fails.

Small new potatoes (or larger ones, cut up, if necessary) 6 to 10
Fresh peas 1½ cups or
    Frozen peas 10-ounce package
Butter 3 tablespoons
Flour 1 tablespoon
Half-and-half or milk 1½ cups
Salt and pepper to taste

1. Peel potatoes and drop into boiling salted water. Cover and cook until almost tender (do not overcook).
2. Add peas and cook until just tender, about 5 minutes. Drain vegetables.
3. Melt butter in saucepan. Stir in flour and cook a minute, until bubbly. Slowly add half-and-half and cook until slightly thickened.
4. Drop in potatoes and peas and combine well, simmering until sauce is desired consistency. Season with salt and pepper and serve.

Italian Beans and Potatoes
Serves 4

Here's a Mediterranean solution to the dinner blahs. Keep it simple by serving it with a fresh tomato salad and a bright, dry Chianti.

Green beans 1 pound (italian or romano beans preferred), cleaned
    and trimmed
Small new potatoes 6 to 8
Salt pork ¼ to ⅓ pound, with rind and salt edge trimmed, minced
Olive oil ⅓ cup
Garlic cloves 4, minced
Salt and pepper to taste

1. Separately, in boiling salted water, cook beans, uncovered, and potatoes, covered, until just tender; drain well.
2. In a large, heavy frying pan slowly brown pork well in oil.
3. Stir in garlic, then beans. Add potatoes. Sauté, gently turning, until vegetables are heated through and flavors are blended. Season with salt and pepper as desired. Serve immediately.

Potatoes in Cream Sauce
Serves 6

This dish, under various aliases, finds its way into just about every cuisine. The universal result is a creamy, "melt-in-your-mouth" side dish that is easy to prepare and very versatile.

Small new potatoes   8 to 9
Butter   4 tablespoons
Cream   ½ cup
Salt and pepper   to taste

1. Scrub potatoes and drop into boiling water to cover for about 12 minutes. (They should be about half-cooked.) Peel potatoes when they are cool enough to handle.
2. Melt butter in top of double boiler. Add potatoes and cream. Cook over barely steaming water for about 30 minutes or until cream is absorbed, stirring occasionally.
3. Season to taste. Remove pan from heat, but keep upper portion of double boiler over warm water in lower portion until ready to serve.
Variations: This dish lends itself readily to interesting variations. Try adding 1 teaspoon of caraway seeds, simmering long enough for seeds to soften, or sprinkle with sweet paprika or with freshly grated parmesan cheese just before serving.

Potatoes Paprika
Serves 4 to 6

Simmered in a delicious broth, these potatoes make an irresistible side dish, or with the addition of smoked sausage an impressive entrée for lunch or supper.

Medium boiling potatoes   4
Vegetable oil or lard   2 tablespoons
Onion   1 cup chopped
Garlic clove   1 to 2, minced
Hungarian sweet paprika   1 tablespoon
Chicken stock   2 cups
Caraway seeds   ¼ teaspoon
Medium tomato   1, peeled, seeded, and chopped
Large green pepper   1, with seeds and membranes removed,
      finely chopped
Salt   1 teaspoon
Pepper   to taste
Hungarian or smoked sausage   1 pound (optional)
Sour cream   ½ cup

1.   Parboil potatoes for 8 to 10 minutes, then peel and cut into ¼-inch slices.
2.   In a 4-quart saucepan or casserole, heat oil, add onions and garlic, and sauté 8 to 10 minutes until lightly colored. Off the heat, add paprika, stirring until onions are well coated.
3.   Return pan to heat, pour in stock, and bring to a boil. Add caraway seeds, potatoes, tomato, green pepper, salt, and pepper (and sausage, if desired). Bring to a boil, stir, reduce heat, and cover. Simmer for 25 to 30 minutes until potatoes are tender.
4.   Serve in bowls with a dollop of sour cream on each serving.

Hungarian Sour Potatoes
Serves 6 to 8

Creamy new potatoes in a caraway sauce make a lovely accompaniment to pork.

Tiny new potatoes about 30 (or use larger ones halved or quartered, about 18 to 20)
Butter 3 tablespoons
Flour 3 tablespoons
Onion ¼ cup chopped
Cooking liquid from potatoes 2 cups
Caraway seeds 1 teaspoon
Lemon juice 1½ tablespoons
Sugar ½ teaspoon
Sour cream ¼ cup
Salt and pepper to taste

1. Cook potatoes covered in boiling salted water until just tender, about 20 to 30 minutes. Drain and reserve cooking liquid. Shake potatoes in saucepan over low heat until they are dry. (Steam will cease to appear.)
2. Heat butter in a skillet. Whisk in flour and mix until it forms a bubbling roux. Add onions and cook until soft.
3. Add 2 cups reserved potato liquid (add water if necessary to make 2 cups) and stir until thickened. Add potatoes and caraway. Simmer for a few minutes.
4. Add lemon juice, sugar, sour cream, and seasonings. Bring to a boil. Add more water, if necessary, to achieve desired consistency. Serve.

Greek Vegetables with Garlic Nut Sauce
Serves 4

If you enjoy the flavor of garlic, you will love this simple, but sumptuous dish. The sauce is especially rich, so serve with a fresh green salad with an oil and vinegar dressing.

Medium new potatoes   4 to 5
Medium beets   3 to 4
Butter   1 tablespoon
Salt and pepper   to taste
Garlic Nut Sauce

1. Boil potatoes and beets separately, each in their jackets, until just tender (30 to 40 minutes, depending on size). Drain. When cool enough to handle, peel and cut into ¼-inch slices.
2. Arrange potato and beet slices, side by side, in overlapping layers in a small, oven-proof serving dish. Dot with butter (warming in oven if necessary to melt it) and sprinkle with salt and pepper to taste.
3. Serve warmed or at room temperature with Garlic Nut Sauce to spoon on top.

Garlic Nut Sauce

Egg yolks   2
White wine vinegar   2 tablespoons
Lemon juice   1 tablespoon
Garlic cloves   4, peeled
Salt   ½ teaspoon
Olive oil   1 cup
Walnuts or lightly toasted blanched almonds   ½ cup chopped

1. In blender or food processor, combine egg yolks, vinegar, lemon juice, garlic, and salt and process.
2. With machine on low speed, gradually add olive oil in a fine, steady stream, blending until a creamy consistency is achieved.
3. Add nuts and process until sauce is blended and thickened.

Artichoke Hearts Provençal
Serves 4 to 6

A light and lemony dish. Serve hot as a luncheon or dinner side dish or serve cold as an hors d'oeuvre.

Olive oil 3 tablespoons
Water ½ cup
Medium onion 1, chopped
Ripe medium tomatoes 2, chopped
Sugar 1 teaspoon
Lemon juice 2 tablespoons
Salt and pepper to taste
Frozen artichoke hearts 10-ounce package, quartered
New potatoes 2 to 2½ cups cooked and diced
Parsley 2 tablespoons chopped

1. Mix oil and water in a skillet. Bring to a boil. Add onion and tomatoes. Simmer for a few moments or until tomato disintegrates in liquid.
2. Add sugar, lemon juice, salt, pepper, and artichoke hearts. Cover and simmer for about 20 minutes.
3. Add cooked potatoes. Simmer an additional few moments, gently tossing potatoes until well coated with sauce. Sprinkle with parsley before serving.

Marinated Potatoes and Vegetables
Serves 4

This is a modified Yiddish recipe. A dish that will definitely perk up any roasted meats.

Medium potatoes   2
Medium beets   2
Large carrot   1
Sauerkraut   ½ cup
Large dill pickle   1, sliced
Green onions   2, sliced
Caraway seeds   1 teaspoon
Olive or vegetable oil   2 tablespoons
Salt and pepper   to taste

1. Peel and cook potatoes, beets, and carrots separately; cut into small pieces.
2. Add sauerkraut, pickle, green onions, and caraway seeds.
3. Add oil and mix. Season with salt and pepper to taste. Serve warm or at room temperature.

Himmel und Erde (Heaven and Earth)
Serves 4 to 6

Another homey German country dish, this makes a nice accompaniment to sausages, baked ham, or pork roast.

Sugar   2 teaspoons
Salt   1 teaspoon
Pepper   ¼ teaspoon
Cold water   1 cup
Medium potatoes   4 to 5, peeled and cut into 1-inch cubes
Large tart apple   1, peeled, cored, and thickly sliced
Lean bacon   ¼ pound, cut into ½-inch dice
Medium onion   1, peeled and sliced into thin rings
Cider vinegar   ½ to 1 teaspoon

1. In a heavy skillet, combine sugar, ½ teaspoon salt, and pepper in water. Drop in potatoes and apple and bring water to a boil over high heat. Reduce heat to moderate. Cover skillet tightly and simmer, undisturbed, until potatoes are tender but not falling apart.
2. Meanwhile, sauté bacon over moderate heat until brown and crisp. With a slotted spoon, remove and drain.
3. Add onions to fat remaining in skillet and cook over moderate heat, stirring frequently, for 8 to 10 minues, or until rings are soft and light brown.
4. Just before serving, stir remaining ½ teaspoon of salt and vinegar into potatoes and apple, and taste for seasoning. Transfer entire contents of skillet to a heated bowl and serve topped with onion rings and bacon.

Schnitzen
Serves 6 to 8

Schnitzen is a hearty specialty of the Alsace-Lorraine region of France. The flavors in this combine to make a sweet and salty casserole that is appealing both to eye and palate.

Dried pears 1 cup
Dried apples 1 cup
Sugar ¼ cup
Water 2 tablespoons
Lean bacon 10 ounces, thickly sliced
Meat stock ½ to 1 cup
Medium potatoes 3 to 4
Salt and pepper to taste

1. Soak pears and apples overnight in water to cover. Drain well.
2. Combine sugar and water in small saucepan. Cover and boil until syrup begins to turn golden brown, shaking pan several times. Remove from heat and add fruit, turning to coat all surfaces.
3. Place bacon in dutch oven or large pot. Arrange fruit over top. Dissolve any caramel remaining in pan with small amount of meat stock and add to fruit. Cover and simmer until bacon and fruit are almost tender, about 35 to 40 minutes.
4. Peel and quarter potatoes. Add to pot and sprinkle with salt and pepper. Cover and cook until potatoes are tender, about 30 minutes, adding more stock as necessary (mixture should be moist but not soupy).

Potato-Spinach Casserole
Serves 4

A nice, light mashed potato casserole that is easily prepared in advance.

Large potatoes   2, boiled until tender
Fresh spinach   1 large bunch or
     Frozen spinach   10-ounce package
Cream   2 tablespoons
Butter   2 tablespoons
Egg   1
Jack or swiss cheese   ½ cup grated
Nutmeg   ¼ teaspoon
Salt and pepper   to taste

1.   Preheat oven to 400°.
2.   Drain potatoes and force through ricer or mash by hand.
3.   Cook spinach until tender (or as per directions on package) and drain well.
4.   Combine potatoes and spinach. Add cream, butter, and egg and beat mixture until light and fluffy.
5.   Stir in cheese; add nutmeg, salt, and pepper. Spoon into buttered 1-quart casserole and bake for 15 to 20 minutes. Serve immediately.

Potatoes Romanoff
Serves 6 to 8

The ingredients for this dish are very simple, while the results are as royal as the Romanoff namesake would claim. Once you've tasted this, you'll understand how such potatoes could get a Russian through an otherwise comfortless winter.

Large potatoes*   6, peeled, boiled, and cubed
Large-curd cottage cheese   2 cups
Sour cream   1 cup
Garlic cloves   1 to 2, minced
Salt   1 teaspoon
Green onions   2 to 3, finely chopped
Cheddar cheese   1 cup grated
Paprika   dash

1. Preheat oven to 350°.
2. Boil potatoes until tender, cube, and combine with cottage cheese, sour cream, garlic, salt, and onions.
3. Turn mixture into shallow, buttered casserole and sprinkle grated cheese over top. Sprinkle paprika over top and bake for about 30 minutes. Serve immediately.

* For best results, use a thin-skinned waxy potato, such as a white rose.

Greek Vegetable Casserole (Briami)
Serves 4 to 6

This is one of our favorite discoveries. Fresh vegetables and herbs combine to make a slightly sweet, wonderfully flavored casserole. Serve with roasted or grilled meats or as a vegetarian main dish.

Medium zucchini 2, sliced
Medium potatoes 2 to 3, sliced
Sweet green peppers 2, sliced, with seeds and membranes removed
Garlic cloves 2, minced
Tomatoes 2 cups peeled and chopped
Sugar ½ teaspoon
Medium onions 2, sliced
Salt and pepper to taste
Parsley 2 tablespoons chopped
Fresh dill or fennel 2 teaspoons chopped or
    Dried dill or fennel 1 teaspoon
Olive oil ½ cup
Parsley, dill, or fennel garnish (optional)

1. Preheat oven to 350°.
2. Mix zucchini, potato, and pepper slices. In small bowl, combine crushed garlic, tomatoes, and sugar.
3. Oil an oven-proof dish and arrange some sliced onion on base. Add a layer of zucchini, potatoes, and peppers combined, and top with some tomato mixture. Season with salt and pepper and sprinkle on some of herbs and olive oil. Repeat until all ingredients are used, 3 to 4 layers according to size of dish, finishing with herbs and oil.
4. Cover and cook in moderate oven for 1 to 1½ hours until vegetables are tender, removing cover for last 15 minutes.
5. Garnish and serve immediately.

Balkan Potato Casserole
Serves 4

This is a delicious, delicately flavored dish.

Medium potatoes   3
Eggs   2, lightly beaten
Cottage cheese   1 cup
Sour cream   1 cup
Fresh nutmeg   ¼ teaspoon, grated
Salt and pepper   to taste

1. Preheat oven to 350°.
2. Peel potatoes and slice as thinly as possible.
3. Combine eggs, cheese, sour cream, nutmeg, and salt and pepper in bowl; mix until well blended.
4. Butter a 1½-quart casserole. Cover with alternate layers of potatoes and cheese mixture, starting with potatoes and ending with cheese.
5. Bake 45 minutes or until cheese is set and lightly browned.

Artichoke Potatoes Italienne
Serves 4 to 5

Potatoes and artichokes form a perfect partnership, especially in this delectable Mediterranean casserole. This makes a great holiday side dish.

Medium potatoes   3, peeled and cut into ½-inch cubes
Olive oil   3 tablespoons
Frozen artichoke hearts   10-ounce package, partially cooked until not quite tender
Salt and pepper   to taste
Eggs   3
Bread crumbs   ½ to 1 cup
Parmesan cheese   1 cup, preferably freshly grated

1. Preheat oven to 350°.
2. Parboil cubed potatoes in salted water (about 5 to 10 minutes). Drain and place in 9- by 13-inch baking pan or 2- to 2½-quart casserole dish that has been oiled with 1 tablespoon olive oil.
3. Drain cooked artichoke hearts and add to potatoes, mixing well. Season

with salt and pepper to taste.
4. Sprinkle remaining 2 tablespoons olive oil over mixture. Combine eggs, bread crumbs, and cheese and blend well. Pour over casserole.
5. Bake for about 40 minutes, until potatoes are tender and topping is lightly browned. Serve immediately.

Indonesian Potato Balls
Serves 4 to 6

Unlike other Indonesian dishes, this one is very mild in its seasoning. It provides a perfect use for a variety of leftovers. The coating of egg white gives these a thin, crispy crust.

Cooked meat (shrimp, chicken, ham, beef, or pork)*   1 cup minced
Small onion   1, minced
Garlic cloves   2, minced
Celery   2 tablespoons chopped
Mashed potatoes   2 cups
Eggs   2, separated
Cornstarch   1 tablespoon
Salt and pepper   to taste
Vegetable oil   for deep frying

1. Combine meat, onion, garlic, and celery and blend into mashed potatoes.
2. Whip egg yolks; stir into potato mixture along with cornstarch. Season with salt and pepper to taste.
3. Shape mixture into balls the size of small eggs. Beat egg whites until frothy and dip balls into them.
4. Deep fry until light brown, drain, and serve.
* If you have several meat leftovers, you may wish to combine the other ingredients, divide the dough into separate bowls, then mix in the meats. This makes for a varied and interesting side dish (as well as virtually cleaning out the refrigerator).

Nutmeg Potato Croquettes
Serves 4 to 6 (12 large croquettes)

The nutmeg, parsley, and parmesan used to season these potato croquettes are a great counterpoint to any roasted, broiled, or barbecued meats.

Medium potatoes   3 to 4, peeled and chunked
Butter   ¼ cup room temperature
Cream or half-and-half   2 tablespoons
Parsley   2 tablespoons chopped
Salt   ¼ teaspoon
Pepper   ⅛ teaspoon
Nutmeg   ⅛ to ¼ teaspoon
Parmesan cheese   ½ to ¾ cup grated
Flour   ½ cup
Eggs   2, beaten
Fine bread crumbs   1 cup
Oil   for deep frying

1.   Simmer potatoes until very tender but not mushy, about 30 minutes. Drain well. Transfer potatoes to large bowl of electric mixer.
2.   Add butter, cream, parsley, salt, pepper, and nutmeg and beat until smooth. Add cheese, blending well. Let cool, then chill several hours or overnight.
3.   By hand or with a pair of large spoons, form mixture into potato shapes, using about ½ cup for each. Gently dredge in flour, coat with egg, then bread crumbs. Arrange on baking sheet. Chill 1 hour or overnight.
4.   Heat oil for deep frying to 350°. Add croquettes in batches and fry until crisp and browned on all sides, about 4 to 5 minutes. Drain well on paper towels. Serve immediately.

Potatoes Roesti I
Serves 4

A potato classic. Perfect for company at breakfast or brunch.

Large baking potatoes   2, peeled
Salt   ½ teaspoon
Nutmeg   ¼ teaspoon freshly grated
Pepper   to taste
Unsalted butter   1½ tablespoons
Vegetable oil   1½ tablespoons

1. Shred potatoes using grater or food processor. Transfer potatoes to bowl and cover with cold water. Let stand, changing water several times, until water is clear (all excess starch has been removed).
2. Drain potatoes well. Spread evenly over towel and roll up lengthwise to dry. Wipe out bowl. Return potatoes to bowl. Add salt, nutmeg, and pepper and toss lightly.
3. Melt half of butter and oil in heavy 10-inch skillet over high heat. Add potatoes, spreading evenly over bottom of pan. Reduce heat to medium, cover, and cook until potatoes are browned on bottom, about 10 minutes.
4. Gently press top of potatoes with spatula and shake skillet to loosen (lift edges if necessary). Place platter over skillet and invert. Add remaining butter and oil to skillet. Slide potato pancake into skillet and cook until browned, shaking skillet to prevent sticking, about 10 minutes.
5. Invert pancake onto platter and serve immediately.

Potatoes Roesti II
Serves 4 to 6

This version of potatoes roesti comes from German-speaking Switzerland where it is very popular. Since the potatoes are even better cooked the day before, it is a great use for leftovers.

Medium potatoes 4 to 5, boiled in their skins and cooled
Butter 4 tablespoons
Salt ¾ teaspoon
Gruyère cheese ½ to 1 cup grated (optional)
Hot water 1 to 2 tablespoons

1. Peel and shred, or cut potatoes into julienne strips. Heat butter in a large skillet.
2. Gradually add potatoes, salt, and cheese. Cook over low heat, turning frequently with a spatula, until potatoes are soft and yellow.
3. Press potatoes with a spatula into a flat cake. Sprinkle with hot water. Cover, and cook over low heat until potatoes are crusty and golden at the bottom, about 15 to 20 minutes. Shake pan frequently to prevent scorching and, if necessary, add a little more butter to prevent sticking. Turn into a hot serving dish, crusty side up, and serve immediately.

Irish Potato Cakes
Serves 4

Sautéed potato cakes make a versatile side dish for any meal: with ham and eggs for breakfast, with roast beef or baked fish for dinner, or with bacon, kidneys, eggs, and fried tomatoes for a traditional Irish "nice fry" or tea.

Mashed potatoes   2½ cups
Butter   2 tablespoons
Salt   1 teaspoon
Caraway seeds   ½ to 1 teaspoon crushed to release aroma
Flour   ½ cup
Butter and/or bacon fat   for sautéing

1. Combine all ingredients thoroughly. Pat out mixture to about ½ inch thick and cut into small rounds.
2. Heat butter in heavy skillet and add cakes, frying until golden on each side. Keep warm in oven until all are done (or refrigerate remaining unused dough for future use).

Variation: Potato cakes are simple to prepare and easily varied. Try adding your favorite grated cheese or parsley and minced onion. For Gloucestershire Potato Cakes, omit the caraway seeds and add ½ cup grated double gloucester cheese and 1 egg. Combine and prepare as above.

Potato Scones
Serves 4 to 8

For those of you who like gnocchi, dumplings, mashed potatoes, and other such comfort food, these potato "scones" will find a warm place in your hearts. These are a handy brunch side dish and a good accompaniment to a simple beef-vegetable soup.

Medium potatoes   2 to 3
Butter   2 tablespoons, melted
Flour   1 cup, sifted
Salt   ½ teaspoon

1. Boil potatoes in jackets in salted water until tender. Drain and mash until all lumps are smoothed. Add melted butter and stir, then add remaining ingredients and stir until combined. (Like regular scones, you will have to use your hands to form the final dough, but little kneading is necessary.)
2. Pat dough into a ½-inch thick circle on lightly floured board. Cut into 8 pie-shaped wedges.
3. Heat a griddle or large frying pan with low sides over medium heat. Butter pan lightly and cook scones about 4 minutes on each side, or until lightly browned and crisp. Split and serve hot with butter.

Fried Potato Patties
Serves 8 to 10

This recipe hails from the Baltic. The patties are golden and crisp on the outside and contrast nicely with something like cold poached salmon with tarragon green sauce.

Medium baking potatoes   6 to 8, peeled and quartered
Egg   1
Flour   ½ to 1 cup
Salt   2 teaspoons
Butter   4 tablespoons

1. Boil potatoes in salted water until tender. Drain thoroughly and either force through ricer or mash in a bowl.
2. Beat in egg, ½ cup flour, and salt, and continue to beat well until mixture is smooth and dense enough to hold its shape in a spoon. (Add remaining flour, 1 tablespoon at a time, if mixture does not hold its shape at this point.)
3. Gather potato dough into a ball, place on a heavily floured surface, and pat it into a thick rectangle. Pat mixture into a larger rectangle, about 1 inch thick, dusting frequently with flour to prevent sticking. Cut 2-inch-wide strips down length of dough, then slice diagonally into 2½-inch-wide lengths. Gently score top of each diamond-shaped patty by making shallow lines down its length.
4. Melt 2 tablespoons butter in heavy skillet set over high heat. When foam has almost subsided, add 6 or 8 patties and brown 3 to 5 minutes on each side, turning carefully with large spatula. Transfer patties to serving platter and cover loosely with foil to keep them warm while you fry the remaining patties, adding more butter to pan as needed.

Pine Nut Potato Cakes
Serves 4

The toasted pine nuts in these potato cakes impart a richness that will send you back for more.

Pine nuts   1 cup, toasted
Onion   2 tablespoons finely chopped
Butter   2 to 3 tablespoons
Mashed potatoes   2 cups
Egg   1
Salt   ½ teaspoon

1. Preheat oven to 350°.
2. To toast nuts, spread nuts evenly on cookie sheet and place in oven, removing when golden (about 5 to 10 minutes).
3. Sauté onion in 1 tablespoon butter until browned. Remove onion from pan and place in mixing bowl.
4. Add nuts, potatoes, egg, and salt to onion and mix well. Shape into 8 flat cakes about ½ inch thick. Brown on both sides in 2 tablespoons butter (or more as needed) in a heavy skillet. Serve immediately.

Sautéed Potato Pancakes with Egg and Onion
Serves 8

These could be the heart of an excellent brunch. Just provide several topping alternatives—sour cream, homemade applesauce, and mushroom sauce—and you'll please any palate.

Medium waxy potatoes   4 to 6, peeled
Small onion   1, peeled
Eggs   2
Salt   1½ teaspoons
Pepper   to taste
Fresh parsley   1 tablespoon chopped
Peanut oil   5 tablespoons

1. Finely grate potatoes and then onion, either in a food processor or by hand. Squeeze vegetables dry in a strong kitchen towel and mix in a bowl with eggs, seasonings, and parsley.
2. Heat oil in a large skillet set over medium-high heat. Add potato mixture to pan by tablespoonfuls, flattening each into a neat oval shape with the back of a spoon or metal spatula, and taking care not to crowd skillet.
3. Sauté pancakes for 2 to 3 minutes on each side, until they are crisp and nicely brown. As they are done, remove them to absorbent paper to drain, and then keep warm on a platter. The sooner they are eaten the better they will be.

Baked Potato Raclette
Serves 4

This baked potato recipe has the variety and character of a complete casserole within a potato skin. A flavorful treat for brunch or as a side dish.

Medium baking potatoes   2
Small mild white onion   1, thinly sliced
Prepared italian dressing   ¼ cup
Bacon strips   5 to 6, cooked, drained, and crumbled
Swiss cheese   ¾ to 1 cup shredded
Butter   2 tablespoons
Diced green chilies   ½ can (4 ounces), well drained

1. Preheat oven to 400°.
2. Scrub potatoes well; pat dry. With a fork, prick skin in several places. Bake in oven for about 1 hour.
3. While potatoes are baking, place onion slices in a bowl. Pour salad dressing over onions and set aside at room temperature. Prepare bacon and shred cheese and set aside.
4. Split cooked potatoes lengthwise and place on a rimmed baking sheet. With a fork, lightly mash each potato half in its skin and mix in butter and chilies. Spoon onion slices and dressing evenly over each, then sprinkle each with bacon and finally cheese. Broil 4 to 6 inches from heat for about 2 minutes or until cheese is melted. Serve at once.

Potatoes in Buttermilk
Serves 4

As a brunch or breakfast dish, this has quickly become a favorite. And like most favorites, it is simple to prepare, unembellished, and a slight twist on the usual.

Butter   2 tablespoons
Potatoes   2 cups peeled and chopped
Salt   ½ teaspoon
Pepper   ⅛ teaspoon
Buttermilk   1 cup
Paprika   garnish

1. Melt butter in skillet; add raw potatoes and toss and cook until potatoes begin to brown.
2. Add salt, pepper, and buttermilk; simmer slowly until potatoes are tender and liquid thickened. (Be careful not to overheat in order to prevent buttermilk from separating and curdling.)
3. Sprinkle paprika on each serving.

Country-Style Ham Hash
Serves 4

This makes a satisfying breakfast or brunch dish, especially when topped with a fried or poached egg.

Vegetable oil   3 tablespoons
Onion   ¼ cup finely minced
Celery   ¼ cup finely minced
Green pepper   ¼ cup finely minced (optional)
Cooked ham   2 cups finely minced
Mashed potatoes   1 cup
Worcestershire sauce   1 teaspoon
Salt and pepper   to taste

1. Heat oil in saucepan. Add onion, celery, and green pepper and sauté until tender but not brown.
2. Mix together ham, potatoes, and worcestershire with sautéed vegetables. Add salt and pepper to taste.
3. Place mixture in refrigerator to chill thoroughly. Shape ham hash into 8 round cakes about ½ inch thick. Brown on both sides in lightly greased griddle or heavy frying pan and serve.

Entrées

Roslfleysch
Serves 6 to 8

Roslfleysch is an example of Jewish cooking at its most basic. Easy to prepare with its few ingredients, the result is hearty and surprisingly tasty. The flavor is reminiscent of sauerbraten.

Chuck steak or fillets   3 to 4 pounds
Large onions   2, sliced
Garlic cloves   2, minced
Vegetable oil   3 tablespoons
Wine vinegar   2 tablespoons
Brown sugar   1 tablespoon
Salt   ½ teaspoon
Bay leaves   2
Water   ½ cup
Medium potatoes   4, quartered

1.   In a large dutch oven, brown meat, onions, and garlic in oil.
2.   Add all remaining ingredients except potatoes. Cover; reduce heat. Simmer for 1 hour.
3.   Add potatoes. Simmer covered 1 hour longer, or until meat is tender.

Hungarian Goulash
Serves 6 to 8

The name "goulash" comes from "gulyas," a Hungarian word originally meaning cattle or sheep herder. At least as far back as the ninth century, these herders were known to have cut meat into cubes, stewed it with onions and spice, and served it as a meal in itself. Today's version is similar in its simplicity to that early dish and remains a dining favorite.

Large onion   1, chopped
Garlic clove   1, minced
Vegetable oil   3 tablespoons
Lean beef chuck   1½ to 2 pounds, cut into ¾-inch cubes
Medium tomatoes   3, chopped
Medium green peppers   1 to 2, chopped, seeds and membranes removed
Hungarian paprika*   1 tablespoon
Caraway seeds   1 teaspoon
Salt and pepper   to taste
Warm water   4 to 5 cups
Medium potatoes   4, peeled and cubed

1. In a large dutch oven, sauté onion and garlic in oil until translucent, stirring occasionally.
2. Brown meat with onions and garlic.
3. Add tomatoes, peppers, paprika, caraway seeds, salt, and pepper. Mix well. Reduce heat to simmer, add 3 to 4 cups water, cover, and cook for 1 hour.
4. Add potatoes to goulash after first hour, along with 1 more cup warm water. Cover and simmer for 30 minutes or until potatoes are tender.
5. Correct seasonings. Serve hot.
* Hungarian paprika is much more flavorful than the mild American type; it lends an authentic touch to this goulash.

Baked Potatoes with Creamed Chipped Beef
Serves 4

A homey dish for lunch or supper—and one that may have plenty of childhood associations.

Dried chipped beef   1 cup
Butter   4 tablespoons
Flour   4 tablespoons
Warm milk   1 cup
Mustard   ½ teaspoon
Cream   ½ cup
Salt and pepper   to taste
Baked potatoes   4
Butter   to taste
Parsley   garnish (optional)

1. Cover chipped beef with boiling water and let stand 5 minutes. Drain and cut into strips. Set aside.
2. Melt 4 tablespoons butter in saucepan, whisk in flour, and cook until well blended. Slowly stir in warm milk. When sauce begins to thicken, add mustard, cream, and salt and pepper. Simmer, stirring often until sauce is thickened and smooth. Add chipped beef.
3. Split freshly baked potatoes and transfer to serving plates. Add a pat of butter to each. Spoon creamed chipped beef over top and sprinkle with chopped parsley. Serve with additional butter on the side.

Potato Gnocchi with Veal Sauce
Serves 4 to 6

*Italian cuisine has produced dishes that we all know and love—ravioli,
spaghetti, tortellini, lasagna. But gnocchi ranks near the top. These dumplings are the kind of comfort food you hope will magically appear on your
dinner table some cold and rainy night.*

Veal Sauce
Warm mashed potatoes*   3 cups
Flour   1½ cups
Salt   1½ teaspoons
Olive oil   1 tablespoon
Eggs   2, slightly beaten
Water   12 cups, salted
Butter   2 to 3 tablespoons, melted
Parmesan, dry jack, or teleme cheese   1½ cups shredded

1. Prepare Veal Sauce.
2. Place potatoes in bowl, add flour, salt, and oil, and blend with a fork.
    Add eggs and blend thoroughly into potato mixture. Turn dough out
    onto floured board and knead gently about 15 times. Shape into a fat
    loaf and set on a floured area to prevent sticking.
3. Cut off one piece of dough at a time (about ½ cup's worth) and roll on
    a very lightly floured board into a cord ⅜ inch thick. Cut cord in
    1¼-inch lengths. Roll each segment in the center lightly under your
    forefinger to give the piece a bow shape. Set shaped gnocchi aside on a
    lightly floured baking sheet; pieces should not touch.
4. When all dough is shaped, cook gnocchi by dropping about a third of
    them at a time into about 3 quarts boiling salted water. Cook for 5
    minutes after they return to surface of water (stir gently if they haven't
    popped up in about 1 minute). Keep water at slow boil.
5. Remove cooked gnocchi from water with slotted spoon, draining well.
    Place cooked gnocchi in shallow-rimmed pan (such as a jelly-roll pan)
    and mix gently with melted butter. Cover tightly with foil and keep in
    warm place while you cook remaining gnocchi. (You can hold gnocchi
    in 150° or lower oven for as long as 3 hours, keeping them well covered
    to retain moisture. Flavor is best if they don't cool after cooking.)
6. To serve, arrange a layer of about half of gnocchi in a wide, shallow-
    rimmed, oven-proof dish, and top with about half of Veal Sauce and

half of cheese. Top with remaining gnocchi, sauce, and cheese. Heat in 375° oven for about 10 minutes or until cheese melts and gnocchi are piping hot. Broil top lightly.

* To make mashed potatoes, cook peeled potatoes until tender in unsalted boiling water and drain thoroughly; then rub through fine wire strainer. Add no other seasonings or ingredients.

Veal Sauce
Makes 4 cups

Dried italian mushrooms ½ cup
Warm water 1 cup
Bacon ¼ cup minced
Olive oil 3 tablespoons
Fat-free boneless veal ¾ pound
Medium onion 1, minced
Carrot 1, finely diced
Celery stalks 2, finely chopped
Tomato sauce 8-ounce can
Whole tomatoes and liquid 16-ounce can
Dry red wine 1 cup
Salt 1½ teaspoons
Allspice ¼ teaspoon
Pepper dash

1. Combine dried mushrooms with warm water and let stand at least 30 minutes.
2. Place bacon in large frying pan with olive oil. Finely chop veal and add to fat in pan along with onion, carrot, and celery. Cook over medium heat, stirring, until vegetables are soft.
3. Drain mushrooms, rinse in water, and drain again; add to meat mixture. Add tomato sauce, whole tomatoes and liquid (break tomatoes apart in pan), wine, and seasonings.
4. Simmer 2 hours, uncovered, or until sauce is reduced to about 4 cups. (Sauce can be made ahead a day or so and stored, covered, in refrigerator.)

Croatian Potato Dumplings with Meat Filling
Serves 5 to 8 (Makes about 16 medium-large dumplings)

Plump, soft dumplings with meat filling and a delicate sour cream–mushroom sauce make a delectable entrée.

Bacon   ½ cup cut into ½-inch strips
Small onion   1, chopped
Ground meat   1 cup
Large baking potatoes   2, cooked and mashed
Butter   2 tablespoons
Eggs   4
Salt   ¼ teaspoon
Flour   2½ cups
Parsley   1 tablespoon minced (optional)
Salt and pepper   to taste
Mushroom Sauce
Butter   1 to 2 tablespoons
Bread crumbs   ½ cup

1. Fry bacon until lightly browned. Remove all but 1 teaspoon fat and add chopped onion. Sauté until onion is transparent, then add ground meat and brown. Remove from heat and set aside.
2. Prepare mashed potatoes. Add butter, 2 eggs, and salt. Mix well. Add 2 to 2½ cups flour to make a fairly stiff dough.
3. Turn dough onto a heavily floured board and roll out to between ⅛ and ¼ inch thick, sprinkling with flour to prevent sticking. Cut into squares about 2½ inches per side.
4. Beat 2 eggs well and stir into meat mixture along with chopped parsley. Season with salt and pepper.
5. Place about 1 tablespoon of meat mixture in center of each square, pull up the corners, and shape into a ball. Roll lightly in flour and place on waxed paper until all dumplings are complete.
6. Prepare Mushroom Sauce.
7. Melt 1 to 2 tablespoons butter and add bread crumbs. Sauté slowly until lightly browned. Set aside.
8. Drop dumplings into boiling salted water and simmer until dumplings rise to top (8 to 12 minutes).
9. Drain dumplings. Serve with a ladle of sauce and a sprinkling of browned bread crumbs.

Mushroom Sauce
Makes 1 cup

Butter 2 tablespoons
Onion ½ cup thinly sliced
Mushrooms ½ pound thinly sliced
Flour 1½ tablespoons
Lemon juice 1 to 2 tablespoons
Chicken broth ½ cup
Sour cream ½ cup
Parsley 1 tablespoon chopped
Salt and pepper to taste

1. Melt butter and add onion. Sauté until transparent, then add mushrooms and sauté until browned (about 5 minutes).
2. Stir in flour and allow to brown. Add lemon juice, chicken broth, sour cream, and parsley, stirring constantly until slightly thickened. Season with salt and pepper to taste and ladle over dumplings.

Scalloped Meat and Potatoes
Serves 6 to 8

A home-style meal-in-one that owes its savory simplicity to French country cooking.

Bacon ½ pound
Ground beef 1 pound
Medium potatoes 6 to 8, sliced into ¼-inch slices
Garlic cloves 4 to 6, minced
Thyme 2 teaspoons crushed
Bay leaves 1 teaspoon crushed
Pepper to taste
Whole bay leaves 3 (optional)
Beef stock 1 cup

1. Preheat oven to 375°.
2. Cook bacon in skillet until almost crisp. Add ground beef and crumble. Cook until all pink is gone, stirring often.
3. Layer about a fifth of potatoes in a 4-quart casserole. Top with a quarter of the meat mixture, some garlic and thyme, crushed bay leaves, and pepper. Repeat layering, ending with potatoes and seasonings.
4. Lay whole bay leaves on top, if desired. Pour stock over casserole.
5. Bake covered tightly for 1¼ to 1½ hours, until potatoes are tender.

Swedish Meatballs
Serves 4 to 6

These are unusual, subtly flavored meatballs. They form a crispy outer shell while staying soft inside.

Onion   3 tablespoons finely chopped
Butter   1 tablespoon
Mashed potato   ¾ cup
Dry bread crumbs   3 tablespoons
Lean ground beef   ¾ to 1 pound
Cream   2 tablespoons
Salt   ½ teaspoon
Egg   1
Parsley   1 tablespoon finely chopped
Nutmeg   ¼ teaspoon
Butter   1 to 2 tablespoons
Vegetable oil   1 to 2 tablespoons
Flour   1 tablespoon (optional)
Cream   ½ cup (optional)

1. Sauté onions in butter for about 5 minutes, until they are soft and trans-lucent but not brown.
2. In a large bowl, combine onion, mashed potato, bread crumbs, meat, 2 tablespoons cream, salt, egg, parsley, and nutmeg. Knead mixture or beat with a wooden spoon until mixture is smooth and fluffy.
3. Shape into small balls about 1 inch in diameter. Arrange meatballs in a layer on a baking sheet or flat tray, cover with plastic wrap, and chill for at least 1 hour before cooking.
4. Melt remaining butter and vegetable oil in a heavy skillet. When foam subsides, add meatballs, 8 to 10 at a time. Reduce heat to moderate and fry balls on all sides, shaking pan frequently. Meatballs should be brown outside and show no trace of pink inside after 8 to 10 minutes of cooking. Add more butter and oil to skillet as needed and transfer each finished batch to a casserole or baking dish and keep warm in a 200° oven. Serve with gravy if desired.

Note: To make a gravy with the pan juice from the meatballs, remove the pan from heat, pour off fat, and stir in 1 tablespoon flour. Quickly add ½ cup cream and boil sauce over moderate heat for 2 to 3 minutes, stirring constantly, until thick and smooth.

Corned Beef Hash with Eggplant and Tomato
Serves 6 to 8

Eggplant, tomatoes, and parmesan cheese provide a slightly Mediterranean twist to this dish that elevates it from a breakfast meal to a buffet entrée.

Small eggplant   1
Salt and pepper   to taste
Flour   ½ cup, approximately
Eggs   2, beaten
Paprika   ¼ teaspoon
Salad oil   for frying
Butter   2 tablespoons
Medium onion   1, finely minced
Large tomatoes   2
Cooked corned beef   1½ to 2 pounds, thinly sliced
Potatoes   3 to 4 cups, boiled and diced
Worcestershire sauce   1 teaspoon or to taste
Lemon juice   1 tablespoon or to taste
Cream   1 cup
Salt and pepper   to taste
Salt   to taste
Parmesan cheese   ½ cup grated

1.   Preheat oven to 375°.
2.   Peel eggplant, cut into thin slices, and sprinkle lightly with salt and pepper. Dip in flour, coating thoroughly. Beat eggs and paprika together. Heat oil ¼ inch deep in a large skillet over medium-high heat. Dip sliced eggplant in eggs, then sauté until brown and tender. Drain and set aside.
3.   In small saucepan, melt butter and sauté onion until tender.
4.   Cut tomatoes into thin slices, allowing as many tomato slices as there are slices of eggplant. Cut corned beef into ⅛-inch dice.
5.   In large mixing bowl, combine corned beef, onion, potatoes, worcestershire, lemon juice, and cream. Mix very well, adding salt and pepper to taste.
6.   Turn corned beef mixture into lightly greased, shallow casserole. Place overlapping alternate slices of eggplant and tomato on top. Sprinkle lightly with salt and cheese. Bake 30 to 40 minutes until top is browned.

Deluxe Corned Beef Hash
Serves 4 to 6

Here is a prince among hashes, suitable for a company breakfast or lunch.

Butter   ½ cup (unsalted preferred)
Small onion   1, finely chopped
Medium potatoes   2, peeled and diced
Cooked corned beef   1 to 1½ pounds, minced
Chicken stock   1 cup
Worcestershire sauce or steak sauce   3 tablespoons
Thyme   ½ teaspoon
Horseradish   1 to 2 teaspoons
Salt and pepper   to taste
Poached or fried eggs   1 per person

1. Preheat oven to 350°.
2. Melt butter in large, oven-proof skillet over medium heat. Add onion and cook until transparent, about 5 minutes. Add potato and sauté until partially cooked, about 5 minutes.
3. Blend in corned beef, stock, worcestershire, thyme, and horseradish. Season with salt and pepper. Bake until most of stock has evaporated, about 30 minutes.
4. Transfer to bowl and let stand until cool. Cover and refrigerate overnight.
5. Press hash mixture evenly into 12-inch nonstick skillet. Place over medium heat and fry until bottom of hash is crisp. Turn over and continue frying until browned on other side.
6. Divide hash among heated plates, spooning into oval shape. Top each with a fried or poached egg and serve.

Hidden Hash
Serves 6

This delicious casserole is a family favorite of Yorkshire-born Pauline Michela. Her formula for a perfect, fluffy Yorkshire pudding on top is to make sure that all the ingredients for it are at room temperature. This is definitely very traditional, very substantial British fare.

Onion   ½ cup chopped
Garlic clove   1 to 2, minced
Butter   1 tablespoon
Potatoes   1 cup diced
Carrot   ½ cup diced
Celery   ½ cup diced
Salt   ½ teaspoon
Pepper   ¼ teaspoon
Beef broth   2 cups
Cooked meat   1 cup diced
Flour   1 to 2 tablespoons
Yorkshire Pudding

1. Preheat oven to 425°.
2. Brown onion and garlic in butter in a large frying pan. Add vegetables. Add salt and pepper and broth and simmer until vegetables are barely soft, about 25 to 30 minutes.
3. Add diced meat. Blend flour with a little cold water and thicken broth and meat mixture to gravy consistency.
4. Turn into buttered baking dish, either 9-inch square or 8-inch square. Cover with Yorkshire Pudding and bake for 30 minutes or until golden and puffed high.

Yorkshire Pudding

Flour   1 cup
Baking powder   ½ teaspoon
Salt   ½ teaspoon
Eggs   2, room temperature
Milk   1 cup, room temperature
Butter   2 tablespoons, melted

1. Sift flour. Sift again 3 times with baking powder and salt.
2. Beat eggs well. Add milk and add to dry ingredients. Beat with egg beater or mixer for 1 minute or until large bubbles form over surface.
3. Add melted butter, mix, and pour over meat mixture.

Hamburger Pie
Serves 4 to 6

Hamburger pie is the kind of food that's comfortable and cozy like a warm fire on a cold winter day. The ingredients are flexible—it's basically just an excuse to combine meat and seasonings with your favorite vegetables and top them with a blanket of mashed potatoes. Use any leftovers that sound interesting or try some completely original combinations. The possibilities are boundless. Here's one good combination to start you on your way.

Onion   1, chopped
Garlic cloves   2, minced
Olive or vegetable oil   1 tablespoon
Hamburger   1 pound
Oregano   ½ teaspoon
Worcestershire sauce   1 tablespoon
Oatmeal*   1 tablespoon (optional)
Mushrooms   ¼ pound, sliced
Small zucchini   2, sliced
Medium tomatoes   2, sliced
Mashed potatoes   2 cups (with milk, butter, and seasoning)
Parmesan or cheddar cheese   ½ cup grated

1. Preheat oven to 375°.
2. Sauté onion and garlic in oil until just turning color. Add hamburger, breaking it up as it browns.
3. Add oregano, worcestershire, and oatmeal while meat is still pink. Stir and continue cooking until meat is done.
4. Using a slotted spoon, remove meat mixture and place in the bottom of a 3-quart casserole. Top with a layer of mushrooms, zucchini, and tomato slices. Cover all with a smooth blanket of mashed potatoes.
5. Sprinkle with grated cheese and bake for about 40 minutes or until edges are turning brown.

* Oatmeal is used to soak up excess fluid. Omit if you prefer a "soupier" version.

Farmhouse Plate Pie
Serves 4

In the past, this recipe was a part of an English farmer's "ordinary"—the meal served on market day in the market town. Typically, this meal began with a hearty soup, followed by a savory pie or pudding with roast meat and abundant vegetables, and finally a dessert and plenty of cheese. Perhaps our appetites are pale imitations of that of the nineteenth-century farmer, but this dish seems a complete meal in itself, served with a fresh green salad.

Medium onion   diced
Medium carrot   diced
Mushrooms   ¼ cup sliced
Oil   2 tablespoons
Cooked meat   1½ to 2 cups chopped or minced
Salt and pepper   to taste
Flour   1 to 2 tablespoons
Beef stock   2 cups
Mashed potatoes   3 cups
Butter   1 tablespoon
Cheddar cheese   ¼ to ½ cup grated

1. Preheat oven to 400°.
2. Dice onion and carrot in ½-inch cubes. Slice mushrooms. Heat oil and sauté vegetables slowly until just tender.
3. Add chopped meat; salt and pepper to taste. Stir in 1 tablespoon flour and cook until bubbly and blended. Pour in stock and simmer, stirring often, until sauce has consistency of medium-thick gravy. (If sauce is too watery, ladle out some sauce and mix with additional tablespoon of flour. Whisk together and return to pan, cooking until thickened.) Remove from heat and set aside.
4. Press half of mashed potatoes into an 8-inch square, greased oven-proof dish or a 9-inch pie pan, being sure to cover sides as well as bottom of pan. Spoon meat and gravy mixture into center. Pat remaining potatoes over top, as evenly and flat as possible. Seal edges and brush top with melted butter. Sprinkle cheese on top.
5. Bake for 30 to 40 minutes, until edges of potato topping are golden.

Iraqi Potato Cakes
Serves 4 to 6

Potatoes are relative newcomers to Iraq and are not available year-round. Thus, these cakes are seasonal and make a special appetizer or luncheon dish. Serve with a salad of romaine, cucumber, tomato, and onion with a vinaigrette. The fillings are somewhat exotic and spicy, but we find most Westerners enjoy them immensely.

Medium potatoes   4 to 5, boiled
Large egg   1, beaten
Flour   ¼ cup
Salt and pepper   to taste
Meat Filling or Vegetable Filling
Flour   ½ cup
Oil   for shallow frying

1. Mash potatoes to a smooth puree. Leave to cool.
2. Blend in egg, flour, and salt and pepper to taste.
3. Make Meat or Vegetable Filling.
4. Take about 1 tablespoon potato mixture and flatten in palm of hand. Put 1 teaspoon filling in center and close potato around filling. Roll into a ball and place on a tray. During shaping, moisten hands with water to prevent potato sticking.
5. Roll balls in flour and flatten to make thick cakes. Arrange on a tray.
6. Place oil in frying pan to depth of ¼ inch. Heat well and fry potato cakes until golden brown on each side—about 3 minutes in all. Drain on paper towels and serve hot, piled on a plate. Garnish as desired.

Meat Filling

Medium onion   1, finely chopped
Oil   1 tablespoon
Garlic clove   1, minced
Ground lamb or beef   8 ounces
Baharat*   1 teaspoon or
    Allspice with dash of pepper and paprika   1 teaspoon
Salt   to taste
Peeled tomatoes   ½ cup chopped
Parsley   ¼ cup chopped

1. Gently fry onion in oil until transparent.
2. Add garlic and ground meat and stir over high heat until mixture is crumbly and meat begins to brown.
3. Stir in spices, salt to taste, tomatoes, and parsley. Reduce heat, cover, and simmer for 15 minutes. Mixture should be fairly dry when cooked.

*Baharat
Makes 1 cup

Black peppercorns   ¼ cup
Coriander seeds   2 tablespoons
Cinnamon bark   2 tablespoons
Cloves   2 tablespoons
Cumin seeds   3 tablespoons
Cardamom seeds   1 teaspoon
Whole nutmeg   2 or
    Ground nutmeg   2 tablespoons
Paprika   ¼ cup

1. Place spices (except nutmeg and paprika) in grinder or blender and grind to a fine powder.
2. Grate nutmeg and add. Blend in paprika. Store in an airtight jar.

Vegetable Filling

Large onion   1, finely chopped
Oil   2 tablespoons
Turmeric   1 teaspoon
Tomatoes   2
Parsley   ½ cup finely chopped
Salt and pepper   to taste

1. Gently fry onion in oil until transparent, add turmeric, and fry for 1 additional minute. Remove from heat.
2. Peel tomatoes, halve crosswise, and remove seeds and juice. Chop finely and place in a bowl.
3. Add onion mixture, parsley, and salt and pepper to taste.

Lemon Lamb with Potatoes
Serves 6

Tender, tangy chunks of lamb alternate with layers of potato slices in a richly flavored sauce. Easily prepared in advance, this Middle East–inspired dish needs only a fresh salad, a light red wine, and some pita bread to round out the meal.

Lemon juice   ¼ cup
Vegetable oil   1 tablespoon
Large garlic clove   1, minced
Coriander seeds   ¼ teaspoon ground
Pepper   pinch
Lamb (from neck, shoulder, or shank)   1½ to 2 pounds, cut into 1-inch
     cubes, with excess fat removed
Butter and vegetable oil   1 tablespoon each
Large onions   2, chopped
Cumin seeds   ⅛ teaspoon
Allspice   pinch
Beef stock   2 cups
Tomato paste   3 tablespoons
Salt   to taste
Medium potatoes   4, boiled until just tender and thinly sliced
Salt   to taste
Fresh cilantro   2 to 3 tablespoons or
     Dried coriander   1 tablespoon crumbled
Fresh lemon juice   2 tablespoons

1. Combine ¼ cup lemon juice, 1 tablespoon vegetable oil, garlic, ground coriander, and pepper in large, shallow dish. Add lamb and stir to coat. Cover and refrigerate 24 hours, stirring mixture occasionally.
2. Remove meat from marinade using slotted spoon; reserve marinade. Pat meat dry. Heat 1 tablespoon each butter and oil in large skillet over medium-high heat. Add lamb in batches and brown on all sides. Transfer lamb to 3- to 4-quart saucepan or dutch oven.
3. Pour off all but thin film of fat from skillet and place over medium-low heat. Add onion and cook until soft, stirring frequently. Blend in cumin and allspice and cook 30 seconds.
4. Add stock, tomato paste, and reserved marinade and bring to a boil, stirring constantly. Pour over lamb. Season lightly with salt. Cover and

simmer gently until lamb is tender, about 1½ hours. (Stew can be prepared ahead and refrigerated for several days.)

5. Arrange layer of potatoes in bottom of greased 1½-quart soufflé or baking dish, overlapping slightly. Sprinkle lightly with salt. Top with half of lamb mixture using slotted spoon. Sprinkle with a third of fresh cilantro and lemon juice. Repeat layering, ending with potato and reserving some cilantro for garnish. Spread sauce over top. (Can be prepared 1 to 2 days ahead to this point and refrigerated. Bring to room temperature before continuing with recipe.)

6. Preheat oven to 350°. Cover baking dish with foil. Bake 30 minutes. Remove foil and continue baking 10 minutes. Sprinkle with remaining cilantro and serve immediately.

Lamb Chops Butcher's Style
Serves 4 to 6

This delicious one-dish meal hails from Greece. The flavor and effect are reminiscent of shish kebabs.

Lamb shoulder chops   6 to 8 (about 2 pounds)
Olive oil   ¼ cup
Salt and pepper   to taste
Oregano   ½ teaspoon crushed
Medium onions   2, sliced
Medium carrots   2, sliced (optional)
Medium tomatoes   4, sliced
Medium potatoes   3, cut into ¼-inch slices

1. Preheat oven to 350°.
2. Trim excess fat from lamb chops.
3. Brush a baking dish with 1 tablespoon oil and place chops in a single layer in dish. Season with salt, pepper, and oregano.
4. Place onions on top of chops, and cover with a layer of sliced carrots and then tomatoes. Season tomatoes lightly.
5. Pour on remaining oil and bake for 50 minutes. Top with potatoes, season lightly, and brush with a little more oil. Return to oven and cook for about 30 additional minutes, or until potatoes are tender.

Pork Loin and Vegetables in Cider
Serves 4 to 6

Succulent pork roast simmered with apples and vegetables in cider makes for a varied and flavorful full meal.

Pork loin roast   3 pounds
Salt and pepper   to taste
Butter   4 tablespoons
Carrot   ½ cup finely chopped
Celery   ½ cup chopped
Leeks   ½ cup chopped
Garlic clove   1, minced
Bay leaf   1
Ground cloves   pinch
Dry cider*   2½ to 3 cups
Medium onions   3 to 4, quartered
Very small new potatoes   10 to 12
Large baking apples   3 to 4, peeled and quartered

1. Preheat oven to 350°.
2. Season pork loin with salt and pepper. Heat 1 to 2 tablespoons butter in a heavy skillet and brown pork on all sides. Remove it and set aside.
3. In the juices remaining in the skillet, sauté carrot, celery, leeks, and garlic over moderate heat for about 10 minutes (do not brown). Put them in bottom of a 5- or 6-quart dutch oven along with bay leaf and cloves. Put pork on top and add enough cider to cover meat halfway.
4. Place covered pot in the center of oven and allow meat to braise for 1 hour and 45 minutes, basting frequently.
5. Add onion wedges and potatoes to pot, adding more cider if necessary to cover them. Cover and return pot to oven for 35 minutes.
6. Melt remaining 2 tablespoons butter in a skillet and brown apple wedges lightly. Add them to pot and bake for another 10 minutes.
7. Remove pork from pot, place it in the center of a platter. Surround with apples, potatoes, and onions; keep warm. Degrease sauce and strain. Pour a little of sauce over meat and vegetables and serve the rest on the side.

* Be sure to get the driest possible cider for this dish. Avoid any sweet ciders.

Braised Pork with New Potatoes and Coriander (Afelia)
Serves 4

This dish originated in Cyprus where coriander is a favored seasoning. It is called an "Afelia," as is any dish combining pork and vegetables with coriander. (If you are not familiar with coriander, try grinding a small amount with mortar and pestle. The fragrance is distinctive, something between mint and eucalyptus.) A chilled green salad with yogurt dressing is a perfect mate to this dish.

Pork fillets or chops 1½ pounds
Butter ¼ cup
Small new potatoes 6, peeled
Small mushrooms ½ pound
Red wine 1 cup
Salt and pepper to taste
Coriander seeds 2 teaspoons crushed

1. Cut pork into 1-inch pieces, leaving some fat with meat for flavor.
2. Heat half of butter in a heavy-bottomed pan and brown potatoes. Remove and set aside.
3. Add remaining butter and brown pork on each side. Push to side of pan.
4. Trim and clean whole mushrooms and fry quickly in pan next to meat. Stir to combine. Reduce heat to low.
5. Pour in wine, add salt and pepper to taste, and place potatoes on top.
6. Sprinkle with crushed coriander, cover pan, and simmer for 45 minutes over low heat or until pork and potatoes are tender. Serve immediately.

Pork and Apple Farmhouse Casserole
Serves 4

*The best farmhouse cooks are wizards at combining basic ingredients with
fresh seasonal produce to create new and delicious variations on a theme.
This casserole is such fare and is especially good with pork—but other
meats will certainly do.*

Medium potatoes   4 to 5, boiled
Butter   2 tablespoons
Medium onion   1, sliced
Sour or tart apples   2, cored and sliced
Cooked pork   1½ to 2 cups chopped or sliced
Salt and pepper   to taste
Nutmeg   freshly grated, to taste
Cream   1 cup

1. Preheat oven to 350°.
2. Slice potatoes in ¼-inch rounds. Heat butter and sauté onion and apple
    slices over medium heat until tender.
3. Grease a 9-inch square oven-proof casserole dish (about 2½ quarts) and
    arrange layers of potatoes, meat, onion, and apples. Season each layer
    with salt, pepper, and nutmeg. Pour cream over top.
4. Bake for about 40 minutes, until bubbly and golden around edges.

Asparagus with Ham and Potato Sauce
Serves 4 to 6

*Adapted from a traditional Dutch recipe (where the sauce is often prepared
by each guest à table), here is a delectable way to celebrate the first tender
asparagus of spring.*

Fresh asparagus   1 pound
Medium new potatoes   2
Eggs   2
Butter   ½ cup
Cooked ham   ½ cup minced
Parsley   ¼ to ½ cup minced
Salt and pepper   to taste

1. Trim, scrape, and steam asparagus until just tender. Drain and keep warm.
2. Peel and quarter new potatoes and boil with eggs until tender (about 10 minutes). Drain, allow to cool slightly, then mash together.
3. Melt half of butter, add ham, and sauté for several minutes. Add parsley, mashed potatoes, and eggs and stir constantly. To blend, add additional butter to thin to desired consistency. Season with salt and pepper and ladle over asparagus spears.

Baked Potatoes with Ham and Mushroom Stuffing
Serves 4

A flavorful stuffing in fluffy twice-baked potato makes an excellent brunch or supper mainstay.

Large baking potatoes 4
Butter   4 tablespoons
Shallots or green onions   2 to 3 tablespoons minced
Medium mushrooms   8, minced
Cream   2 tablespoons
Cooked ham   ½ cup minced
Salt and pepper   to taste
Parmesan cheese   2 tablespoons grated
Olive or vegetable oil   to taste

1. Preheat oven to 400°. Bake potatoes about 1 hour or until soft. Remove and set aside.
2. Melt 2 tablespoons butter in skillet. Add shallots and mushrooms and sauté until vegetables are tender. Set aside.
3. Slice a cap about ¼ inch thick off top of each potato. Remove insides of potatoes carefully with a tablespoon, keeping shells intact (a thin layer of potato should be left in each shell to keep skin from tearing).
4. Mash or put potatoes through potato ricer. Add mushroom mixture, remaining butter, cream, ham, and salt and pepper. Blend well. Stuff mixture back into shells, forming smooth rounds.
5. Sprinkle with cheese and oil and bake at 375° for 25 to 30 minutes. Serve piping hot (with additional butter, if desired).

Ham and Potato Quiche
with Cheddar Shortbread Crust
Serves 6

This recipe combines two of our old favorites—ham and potato quiche and cheddar shortbread. It is a very rich entrée, one that you will want to serve with crisp greens, perhaps a simple stir-fry, and some chilled seasonal fruit with a light yogurt dressing for dessert.

Potatoes   2
Cheddar Shortbread   enough for 1 pie shell
Onions   2, chopped
Cooked ham   ¾ pound, diced
Eggs   3
Half-and-half   1½ cups
Salt   ¼ teaspoon
Pepper   ⅛ teaspoon
Parmesan cheese   2 tablespoons grated
Chopped parsley   garnish
Paprika   garnish

1. Preheat oven to 350°.
2. Boil potatoes in their jackets in salted water for about 10 minutes. Cool, peel (if desired), and cut into thin slices. Spread half of potato slices over bottom of pastry shell. Sprinkle half of onions over slices, then cover with half of diced ham. Repeat once more.
3. Lightly beat eggs with wire whisk. Add half-and-half and seasonings and blend until smooth.
4. Set pastry shell on cookie sheet and carefully pour in custard mixture. Bake on center shelf of oven for 1 to 1½ hours, or until top is puffed up and browned and a knife inserted in center of custard comes out clean.
5. Remove from oven and sprinkle grated parmesan cheese over top. Place under broiler until cheese melts and turns golden brown. Remove and slide onto wire rack to cool for 5 to 10 minutes. Garnish and serve hot.

Cheddar Shortbread
Makes 1 pie shell plus several small wedges

This is a wonderful shortbread that can be patted into a circle, cut into wedges, baked, and served as an appetizer or with soup or salad. As a quiche crust, it is unparalleled.

Butter   1 cup
Sharp cheddar cheese   1½ cups shredded
Flour   2 cups
Salt   1 teaspoon
Cayenne   ⅛ teaspoon

1. In large bowl of mixer cream butter until fluffy. Beat in cheese. Stir in flour, salt, and cayenne.
2. Turn out onto floured surface and knead lightly to blend well (mixture is often crumbly and requires handling to hold together).
3. If using for quiche crust, pat dough into circle about ½ inch thick, then press into deep pie or quiche pan until bottom and sides are covered with about ⅛ inch to ¼ inch of crust (depending on your preference).
4. If using for shortbread wedges, press dough into 10-inch circle and cut into 16 wedges.
5. Quiche crust should be unbaked when filled with custard. Shortbread wedges should be baked on greased cookie sheet in preheated 425° oven 25 minutes or until golden. (Can be served hot or cold.)

Note: You will have extra dough from this recipe if you are making 1 quiche crust. If so, press remainder into ¼-inch width and cut out small shapes. Bake as directed for shortbread wedges, reducing time to approximately 10 minutes.

Scalloped Ham and Potatoes
Serves 4 to 6

This is an excellent meat and potato dish that harkens back to our mothers' traditional meals.

Medium onions   2, thinly sliced
Butter   4 tablespoons
Medium potatoes   4, thinly sliced
Cooked ham   1½ to 2 cups cubed
Flour   3 tablespoons
Salt and pepper   ½ teaspoon each
Sharp cheddar cheese   1½ to 2 cups grated
Paprika   to taste
Milk   1 cup

1.   Preheat oven to 350°.
2.   Sauté onions in 1 tablespoon butter until just tender. Set aside.
3.   Layer half of potatoes and ham in bottom of a 2-quart casserole that has been buttered with 1 tablespoon butter. Combine flour, salt, and pepper and sprinkle half of mixture over potatoes. Top with half of onions and cheese; sprinkle with paprika. Repeat layering.
4.   Scald milk and pour over casserole. Dot with remaining 2 tablespoons butter and bake for 1¼ to 1½ hours, until potatoes are tender and top is golden.

Ham and Potato Casserole
Serves 4 to 6

Here is another variation of an old favorite. This ham and potato dish is lighter and more delicately flavored due to the sweetness of the green pepper and the addition of an egg.

Butter   3 tablespoons
Medium-large potatoes   4, thinly sliced
Medium onions   2, sliced
Medium green peppers   2, seeded and cut into thin strips
Cooked ham   1½ pounds, diced
Egg   1
Milk   1 cup
Salt and pepper   to taste
Jack or cheddar cheese   1 cup grated

1. Preheat oven to 350°.
2. Butter a 2-quart baking dish with 1 tablespoon butter. Cover bottom with a layer of potatoes, top with a layer of onions, a layer of peppers, and a layer of ham. Repeat until dish is filled, ending with a layer of potatoes.
3. Beat egg with milk, season to taste, and pour over casserole. Dot with 2 tablespoons butter and bake for 1½ hours. Sprinkle with cheese and return to oven or place under broiler to brown.

Farmhouse Ham Hock with Beans and Potatoes
Serves 4 to 6

In the farmhouse or an inner city apartment, this economical dish makes a favorite casual meal. The sprinkling of cider vinegar gives it extra pizzazz.

Ham hock   1½ to 2 pounds
Water   1½ to 2 quarts
Fresh green beans   1½ cups trimmed or
   Frozen green beans   9-ounce package
Onion   1, peeled and quartered
Medium new potatoes   4 to 5, quartered
Salt and pepper   to taste
Cider vinegar   to taste

1. Place ham hock in a large pan, cover with water, and bring to boil. Reduce heat, cover pan, and simmer ham for 1½ hours.
2. Add trimmed green beans and simmer for 10 to 15 minutes. (If using frozen beans, add during the last 10 to 12 minutes of cooking time.) Add onion and potatoes and continue to cook for 25 minutes or until potatoes are tender. Season with salt and pepper to taste.
3. Remove ham hock, cool, cut off meat, and chop it finely. Place vegetables in a serving bowl and cover with 1 cup of cooking liquid (mixed with 2 tablespoons of cider vinegar, if desired) and the chopped ham. Serve immediately with a cruet of vinegar to sprinkle over vegetables.

Spanish Potato Pie
Serves 4 to 6

This lively, full-flavored casserole makes a welcome one-dish meal. Like a pizza, it can only improve as you substitute your own variations.

Onion   1, minced
Vegetable or olive oil   2 tablespoons
Mashed potatoes   2 cups
Cooked ham   1 cup diced
Sharp cheddar cheese   ½ cup grated
Pimiento   ½ cup drained and diced
Green olives   ¼ to ½ cup chopped
Garlic clove   1, minced
Artichoke hearts   ½ cup chopped (optional)
Salt and pepper   to taste
Eggs   2, room temperature, separated
Chicken broth or bouillon   ¼ cup
Seasoned tomato sauce   8-ounce can
Mint leaves   ¼ to ½ teaspoon crushed

1. Preheat oven to 350°.
2. Sauté onion in oil until lightly browned.
3. Combine potatoes, onions, ham, cheese, pimiento, olives, garlic, and artichoke hearts with salt and pepper to taste.
4. Beat egg yolks with chicken broth until frothy. Add to mixure.
5. Beat egg whites until stiff and fold into mixture.
6. Pour mixture into round, greased pie dish or casserole. Top with tomato sauce and mint.
7. Bake for about 40 minutes, until pie is browning around edges and is slightly puffed. Let cool for a few minutes before serving.

Variations:
   Substitute ham with chicken or fish or other leftover meats.
   Try with a jack or provolone cheese instead of or in combination with cheddar.
   Replace green olives with ripe black olives.

Country Omelet
Serves 2

This is a wonderfully rich omelet with varied flavors and textures. Perfect for brunch or late night supper.

Bacon strips   4
Walnut halves   8 to 12
Small red or white potato   1, diced
Onion   ¼ cup diced
Butter   2 tablespoons
Eggs   3 to 4
Swiss cheese   ⅓ cup grated
Parsley   1 tablespoon minced
Sour cream   ¼ to ½ cup or
   Crème Fraîche (see Index)   ¼ cup
Salt and pepper   to taste

1. In wide frying pan, cook bacon over medium heat until crisp. Remove bacon from pan, crumble, and set aside.
2. Add walnuts to drippings and cook, stirring, over medium heat for 1 to 2 minutes or until nuts are lightly browned; set nuts aside.
3. Discard all but 2 tablespoons drippings. Add potato and onion and cook, stirring, over medium-low heat until potato is tender but only lightly browned (about 10 minutes); remove from pan, set aside, and keep warm.
4. In a 7- to 8-inch omelet pan over medium-high heat, melt butter and heat until foam begins to subside. Pour in eggs. As edges begin to set, lift with a spatula and shake or tilt pan to let uncooked egg flow underneath.
5. When egg no longer flows freely and top of omelet is still moist, sprinkle eggs with cheese, potato, bacon, and parsley. Remove from heat.
6. Mound sour cream in center of omelet. Garnish with toasted walnuts. Cut into wedges to serve and salt and pepper to taste.

Potato-Sausage Supper
Serves 4 to 6

This is a bountiful one-dish meal that will satisfy any sausage lover.

Sausage 1 pound, thinly sliced
Butter 5 to 6 tablespoons
Medium potatoes 3, cut into ¼-inch slices
Large onion 1, sliced
Celery ½ cup chopped
Dill pickle ½ cup chopped
Dill pickle juice ¼ cup
Sugar 1 teaspoon
Caraway seeds ½ to 1 teaspoon
Dry mustard ½ teaspoon
Salt and pepper to taste
Parsley garnish

1. In a wide frying pan, brown sausage over medium heat. With a slotted spoon, remove and set aside.
2. In same pan, melt 3 tablespoons of butter. Add potato slices, a few at a time, to be sure each slice gets coated with butter, and turn frequently, adding more butter as needed to coat potatoes thoroughly. Add onion and cook, turning often, until onion and potatoes are golden.
3. Gently stir in celery, dill pickle, and browned sausage.
4. Combine pickle juice, sugar, caraway seeds, and mustard; add to potato mixture. Cover, reduce heat to low, and cook for 20 to 25 minutes or until potatoes are tender when pierced; turn often.
5. Season with salt and pepper. Garnish with parsley and serve.

Potato-Corn Pancakes with Sausage-Chile Salsa
Serves 4

This is a spicy entrée that is attractive enough for a special brunch with your potato-loving friends. The hot links or chorizo give this dish its punch, so it is up to you to choose just how spicy it will be.

Flour   2 tablespoons
Salt   1 teaspoon
Pepper   ¼ teaspoon
Eggs   2, separated and brought to room temperature
Cream   ¼ cup
Corn   1 cup, barely cooked
Medium baking potatoes   2, grated
Hot links or chorizo   1 pound
Oil   2 tablespoons
Butter   2 tablespoons
Green chilies   two 4-ounce cans, chopped and well-drained
Salt   pinch
Cream of tartar   pinch
Sour cream or Crème Fraîche (see Index)   1 cup or more

1. Preheat oven to 200°.
2. Combine flour, 1 teaspoon salt, and pepper in large bowl and stir well. Mix egg yolks and cream in small bowl. Gradually stir into flour until just moistened. Stir in corn.
3. Wash grated potatoes (to eliminate starch) until water runs clear. Dry thoroughly in salad spinner or towel. Set aside.
4. Slice sausage into ¾-inch rounds and brown in 1 tablespoon each oil and butter. Add well-drained chilies and heat through. Set aside.
5. Beat egg whites with salt and cream of tartar until stiff but not dry. Add potatoes to corn mixture and blend well. Fold in egg whites. Use batter immediately or it will become watery.
6. Form 3-inch pancakes on griddle or in skillet heated with remaining butter and oil. Fry until bottoms are browned and set, about 5 minutes. Turn and brown second side, pressing pancakes lightly with spatula. To keep warm, arrange in single layer on rack in oven. Repeat with remaining batter, mixing gently before cooking.
7. Arrange pancakes on platter and surround with sausage and chili mixture. (Use slotted spoon if necessary.) Serve with sour cream.

Sausage Supper Pie
Serves 4 to 6

This is the kind of wholesome, unadorned supper dish that one loves to come home to.

Link sausages   1 pound
Medium onions   2, thinly sliced
Medium apples   2, thinly sliced
Flour   1 tablespoon
Chicken stock   1 cup
Salt and pepper   to taste
Mashed potatoes   2 to 2½ cups
Paprika   to taste

1. Preheat oven to 350°.
2. Sauté sausages until brown; drain. Slice each link into ½-inch slices and place in deep, 9-inch pie plate.
3. Pour off all but 2 tablespoons of fat from frying pan. Add onions and apples and simmer slowly until tender; remove from pan with slotted spoon. Blend flour into remaining fat, then add stock, stirring constantly. Simmer until smooth and thick. Return onions and apples to sauce and add salt and pepper to taste.
4. Pour mixture over sausages, spread mashed potato over top, and sprinkle lightly with paprika. Bake until browned, about 30 minutes. Serve hot.

Pigs in Blankets
Serves 3

Great fun and surprisingly tasty. This is good for breakfast, brunch, or even a late night supper.

Oil   for deep-fat fryer
Mashed potatoes   2 cups
Parsley   1 teaspoon minced
Onion   1 teaspoon minced
Egg yolk   1
Bread crumbs   1 cup
Egg   1, slightly beaten (plus additional egg white from above)
Vienna sausages   6 or
    Small pork sausages   6, precooked

1. Preheat deep-fat fryer to 375°.
2. Combine potatoes, parsley, onion, and egg yolk and mix well.
3. Set out 3 shallow bowls: 1 with potato mixture, 1 with bread crumbs, and 1 with egg plus additional white. Coat sausages in potato mixture, patting to shape evenly. Roll in crumbs, then egg, then in crumbs again. (This is easiest to do with the ends of each "piggy" sticking out slightly for use as handles. Also, they look more like pigs in blankets this way.)
4. Fry pigs in blankets, being careful not to crowd them, until they are golden brown. Serve immediately.

Potato, Fontina, and Salami au Gratin
Serves 4 to 6

This is a great buffet dish for company.

Unsalted butter   4 tablespoons
Medium potatoes   4 to 5, boiled, cooled, and peeled
Fontina cheese   ½ cup slivered
Salami   ½ pound, diced
Parsley   ¼ cup chopped
Olive oil   2 tablespoons
Chicken stock   2 tablespoons (optional)
Salt and pepper   to taste
Buttermilk or cream   1 cup
Bread crumbs   ½ cup
Parmesan cheese   ¼ cup grated

1. Preheat oven to 375°.
2. Butter a 2-quart casserole or deep pie dish with 1 tablespoon butter. Set aside.
3. Slice potatoes, then arrange in layers with fontina slivers, salami, parsley, and dots of butter. Sprinkle each layer with olive oil and broth and salt and pepper. End with layer of potatoes.
4. Pour buttermilk over casserole. Mix bread crumbs with parmesan and distribute evenly over top.
5. Bake for about 50 minutes or until potatoes are completely tender and bread crumbs are golden.

Country Chicken Bake
Serves 4 to 6

This is good English "homely" fare—the sort of dish that a country wife would throw together with leftover meat from a newly fattened and butchered hen and fresh leeks from her garden. And topping it off is a light potato pastry crust to please the earthiest eater.

Leeks   4, sliced (white portion only)
Butter   2 tablespoons
Cooked chicken   1 cup sliced
Potato Pastry Crust
Eggs   3
Cream   ½ cup plus 1 tablespoon
Rosemary, thyme, and oregano   pinch of each
Salt and pepper   to taste
Paprika   garnish

1. Preheat oven to 350°.
2. Wash leeks, pat dry, and cut into thin slices. Sauté in butter until limp.
3. Place chicken slices in pastry crust. Arrange sautéed leeks over top.
4. Whisk together eggs and ½ cup cream, season, and pour into pastry shell. Sprinkle paprika over top. Place remaining pastry rounds over top of pie and brush with 1 tablespoon cream.
5. Place pie on cookie sheet and bake for 35 to 40 minutes, or until knife inserted in center of custard comes out clean. Let stand 5 minutes and serve.

Potato Pastry Crust
Makes 2 single crusts

A handy way to use that one lone russet that is sitting in your kitchen, this crust can be used with a variety of vegetable or meat-and-vegetable quiches.

Flour   ¾ cup
Salt   1 teaspoon
Butter   4 tablespoons
Mashed potato   1 cup

1. Mix flour and salt and cut butter into mixture with pastry blender. Stir in mashed potato and mix until dough is formed. Knead dough very slightly on floured board and divide pastry in half.
2. Roll out half of pastry and line an 8-inch pie plate. Prick and leave in a cool place for about 30 minutes. Roll out remainder of dough and cut into rounds with glass or biscuit cutter about 1¾ inches in diameter.

Chicken Pie
Serves 4 to 6

This is a cousin to the Hamburger Pie. Again, here's an opportunity to throw in those artichoke hearts or any other favorite vegetable or seasoning to give this dish a personal touch.

Onion   1, chopped
Garlic cloves   2, minced
Olive or vegetable oil   1 tablespoon
Marjoram   ½ teaspoon crushed
Flour   1 tablespoon
Chicken stock   ¾ cup
Chicken meat   2 cups torn or chopped
Parsley   2 tablespoons chopped
Mushrooms   ¼ pound, sliced
Carrots   1 cup sliced and cooked
Mashed potatoes   2 cups (with milk, butter, and seasoning)
Parmesan or swiss cheese   ½ cup grated

1. Preheat oven to 375°.
2. Sauté onion and garlic cloves in oil until nearly tender. Stir in marjoram and flour and cook a couple of minutes longer.
3. Add chicken stock and cook, stirring often, until sauce has a thick gravylike consistency. Add chicken meat and parsley and mix.
4. Pour mixture into bottom of a 3-quart casserole. Top with a layer of mushrooms, then cooked carrots. Cover with mashed potatoes.
5. Sprinkle with grated cheese and bake for about 40 minutes.

Chicken with Potatoes and Carrots
Serves 4

This combination of crumb-coated, curry-flavored chicken and vegetables baked in their own juices is irresistible. The ingredients are commonplace enough that you are likely to have them on hand for a family meal, while the flavors are special enough to make this a treat for company, too.

Bread crumbs   ¼ cup
Cornmeal   ¼ cup
Curry powder   1½ teaspoons
Salt   ½ teaspoon
Pepper   to taste
Broiler/fryer chicken   3 to 3½ pounds, cut up or in quarters
Butter   ½ cup
Small new potatoes   8
Small carrots   8
Parsley   garnish

1.   Preheat oven to 400°.
2.   Combine crumbs, cornmeal, curry, salt, and pepper in a small bag. Shake each chicken piece in it until completely coated. Set aside.
3.   Put butter in a shallow 3-quart casserole or baking dish and place in oven until butter melts.
4.   Roll potatoes and carrots in butter, tilting pan and turning vegetables to coat evenly. Push to one side. Coat chicken pieces and arrange skin side down with vegetables.
5.   Bake, uncovered, for 50 to 55 minutes, turning chicken and vegetables once after first 25 minutes. Vegetables should be tender when pierced and chicken meat no longer pink near bone. Garnish with chopped parsley and serve.

Oven-baked Chicken with Potatoes and Mushrooms
Serves 4

This is a superb supper dish. You will find your bread chasing any remaining drops of its tangy sauce from one end of your plate to the other!

Chicken   3½ pounds, cut into serving pieces
Salt and pepper   to taste
Olive oil   2 tablespoons
Butter   1 tablespoon
Potatoes   3 cups cut into 1-inch cubes
Mushrooms   6 to 8, quartered
Garlic cloves   3, minced
Marjoram or rosemary   ½ teaspoon
Chicken broth   1 cup
Lemon juice   2 tablespoons
Flour   1 teaspoon (optional)
Parsley   2 tablespoons chopped

1. Preheat oven to 400°.
2. Sprinkle chicken pieces with salt and pepper. Heat oil and butter in large, heavy skillet or dutch oven and add chicken pieces skin side down. Cook over medium heat for 8 to 10 minutes until nicely browned.
3. As chicken cooks, drop potatoes into cold water to cover. Bring to a boil, then drain immediately. Set aside.
4. When chicken pieces are browned, remove from heat, turn pieces skin side up, and scatter potatoes and mushrooms around them, stirring in oil and butter to coat. Add garlic and sprinkle with marjoram. Bake covered for 30 minutes.
5. Add chicken broth and bring to boil on top of stove. Remove chicken pieces to a hot platter. Add lemon juice to sauce. (If you desire a thickened sauce, ladle out some hot sauce, mix with flour, and return to sauce, stirring until slightly thickened.)
6. Serve potatoes and mushrooms in sauce, pouring extra sauce over chicken pieces. Garnish chicken with parsley.

Shellfish-Potato "Lasagne"
Serves 8 to 10

We are great fans of fresh shellfish and we love dishes that are layered. This "lasagne" is a perfect vehicle for both. It is also a bit more expensive than a regular Tuesday night casserole — in fact, it is luxurious enough to save for a birthday, anniversary, or buffet party.

Small waxy potatoes 8 to 10
Garlic cloves 2, minced
Green onions 3, chopped
Butter 5 tablespoons
Mushrooms ½ pound, thinly sliced
Parsley 2 to 3 tablespoons chopped
Bay scallops ½ pound
Dry white wine ½ cup
Flour 4 tablespoons
Cream 2 cups
Nutmeg ½ teaspoon
Salt and pepper to taste
Parmesan cheese ¾ cup grated
Crab ¼ pound
Shrimp ½ pound
Mozzarella cheese 1½ cups thinly sliced

1. Preheat oven to 350°.
2. Boil potatoes in jackets in salted water for 10 minutes or until tender but not done. Slice into thin rounds when sufficiently cool.
3. Sauté garlic and green onions in 1 tablespoon butter until slightly limp. Add mushrooms and parsley and sauté 2 minutes. Remove vegetables to a dish.
4. Poach scallops in wine until opaque, about 3 minutes. Remove scallops with slotted spoon and reserve cooking wine.
5. Melt remaining 4 tablespoons butter in large skillet. Add flour, whisk until smooth, and cook until bubbling and slightly golden. Gradually add cream, reserved scallop poaching wine, and nutmeg. Salt and pepper to taste. Stir constantly until thickened. (If you wish to thin sauce, add additional wine.) Add ¼ cup parmesan and stir until blended.
6. Add sautéed vegetables to sauce and spoon small amount of sauce over bottom of 2½-quart casserole. Place a third of potato slices on bottom, then sprinkle half of scallops, crab, and shrimp over potatoes. Ladle

half of remaining sauce over seafood. Lay a third of mozzarella slices over sauce. Repeat layering, topping with final layer of potatoes, mozzarella, and parmesan.

7. Bake for 30 to 45 minutes. Broil for 2 to 3 minutes after baking time, until cheese topping is golden.

Mussel-Potato Pudding
Serves 4 to 6

Mussels are such a delicate and succulent shellfish that it is always a treat to find them in Seattle's Public Market. While they are certainly outstanding with garlic and tomato sauces, this "pudding" of potatoes and mussels showcases their subtle sea flavor.

Waxy potatoes   4 cups cooked and thinly sliced
Mussel meats   2 cups (about 3 pounds), cooked and drained
Shallots   ¼ cup minced
Butter   1 tablespoon
Cream or half-and-half   2 cups
Eggs   2, beaten
Butter   2 tablespoons, melted
Calvados or applejack*   2 tablespoons
Nutmeg   1 teaspoon
Parmesan cheese   2 to 4 tablespoons
Paprika   garnish

1. Preheat oven to 325°.
2. Butter a 1½-quart shallow baking dish. Arrange a layer of potatoes on bottom, then a layer of mussels. Sauté shallots in 1 tablespoon butter until softened. Sprinkle shallots over potatoes and mussels. Repeat layering, ending with potatoes.
3. Blend cream, eggs, melted butter, Calvados, and nutmeg. Pour over potatoes. Sprinkle with cheese and garnish with paprika.
4. Bake uncovered for 45 to 60 minutes, or until pudding consistency has been achieved.

* Madeira or sherry can be substituted if you prefer a stronger flavor.
Variation: Eliminate Calvados and nutmeg and substitute 1 teaspoon dill seed.

Country Fish Pie
Serves 4 to 6

This version of fish pie is richly flavored and creamy. A salad of sweet red bell pepper, bermuda onion, and red-leafed lettuce tossed in an herbed vinaigrette will complete an already delicious picture.

Cod or other mild whitefish   1 pound
Milk   1¾ cups
Salt and pepper   to taste
Butter   ½ cup
Flour   ⅓ cup
Mushrooms   1 to 1½ cups sliced
Medium tomatoes   3 to 4, chopped
Peeled shrimp   ½ to 1 cup
Lemon juice   1 tablespoon
Sour cream   2 tablespoons
Salt and pepper   to taste
Medium potatoes   4, boiled and mashed (with milk and butter to moisten)

1. Preheat oven to 350°.
2. Put fish in a 10-inch pie plate or a 9-inch-square baking dish with milk and a sprinkling of salt and pepper. Bake for 10 to 15 minutes until fillets are cooked.
3. Remove fish from oven and flake it into small pieces. Be sure to take out any bones. Strain milk in which fish was baked into a small bowl.
4. Melt 4 tablespoons butter in a saucepan. Stir in flour and cook for about 2 minutes, stirring constantly. Gradually add fish liquor and cook over low heat, stirring until sauce is thick and creamy.
5. Sauté mushrooms, tomatoes, and shrimp in 2 tablespoons butter for a few minutes. Add them to sauce along with lemon and sour cream. Season to taste with salt and pepper.
6. Put fish in baking dish and pour sauce on top. Cover with mashed potato. (Do not try to smooth down potato; leave it bumpy.) Dot top with remaining 2 tablespoons butter.
7. Bake for 20 minutes. Then place under broiler for a few minutes until browned. Serve immediately.

Kippered Cod with Potatoes and Capers
Serves 4

This unusual casserole has a smoky and tart combination of tastes. Once you bite into it, you'll be hooked.

Medium-large potatoes   3 to 4, sliced
Butter   4 tablespoons
Large onion   1, thinly sliced
Kippered cod   ½ to ¾ pound or
   Kippered salmon or halibut   ½ pound
Flour   2 tablespoons
Milk   1 to 1½ cups
Paprika   1 teaspoon
Dijon mustard   1 teaspoon
Salt and pepper   to taste
Capers   1 to 2 tablespoons drained and chopped
Lemon juice   2 tablespoons
Parsley   garnish (optional)

1. Preheat oven to 350°.
2. Cook potatoes in boiling salted water just until tender when pierced (about 5 minutes). Drain well and arrange in a shallow, buttered 2-quart casserole or 9-inch-square baking dish.
3. In a wide frying pan, melt 2 tablespoons butter. Add onions and sauté until soft; spoon evenly over potatoes.
4. Flake fish with a fork, discarding skin and bones; distribute evenly over onions.
5. Melt remaining 2 tablespoons butter in frying pan or heavy saucepan. Blend in flour, stirring, until bubbly. Gradually pour in milk and continue cooking and stirring until sauce boils and thickens. Season with paprika, mustard, salt, pepper, capers, and lemon juice. Spoon sauce over fish. (At this point, you can cool, cover, and refrigerate until next day.)
6. Bake, uncovered, for 20 to 30 minutes (35 minutes if refrigerated), until potatoes are tender. Garnish with parsley if desired.

New Potatoes with Baked Fish and Caper Sauce
Serves 4

Flaky white fish and creamy new potatoes make a great team, but when you add this lively caper sauce, the result is irresistible.

Whitefish fillets (cod, halibut, tuna)   2 pounds
Salt and pepper   to taste
Butter   3 to 4 tablespoons, melted
Small new potatoes   12, boiled in their jackets and hot
Caper Sauce

1. Preheat oven to 350°.
2. Wipe fish dry; season lightly with salt and generously with pepper. Arrange in a single layer in a shallow baking dish.
3. Pour butter over. Bake just until flesh barely separates when tested with knife (about 12 to 15 minutes, depending on fish), basting once or twice with pan juices.
4. Lift to serving platter and pour pan juices over. Arrange potatoes alongside. Spoon part of Caper Sauce over both fish and potatoes. Pass remaining sauce.

Caper Sauce

Butter   ½ cup
Capers   1 to 2 tablespoons drained
Parsley   2 tablespoons chopped
Lemon juice   1 teaspoon

1. Melt butter.
2. Add capers, parsley, and lemon juice and barely heat through.

Austrian Eggs
Serves 2

Anchovies and dijon mustard give punch to this hearty one-dish meal. This is a good way to use leftover boiled potatoes and can be served any time of day.

Medium potatoes   2, boiled and sliced
Hard-cooked eggs   2, sliced
Anchovy fillets   2, chopped
Dijon mustard   1 teaspoon
Cream   ⅓ cup
Salt and pepper   to taste
Bread crumbs   2 to 3 tablespoons
Parsley   2 tablespoons finely chopped
Parmesan cheese   2 tablespoons grated
Butter   1 to 2 tablespoons

1. Preheat oven to 350°.
2. Butter 2 ramekins or a small baking dish. Arrange potatoes and eggs in layers and top with anchovies.
3. Combine mustard and cream and pour over potato mixture. Season with salt and pepper to taste.
4. Combine remaining ingredients and scatter on top. Bake for 20 minutes.

Cauliflower Mushroom Pie with Grated Potato Crust
Serves 4 to 6

This wonderfully seasoned vegetable entrée is among the best we've tasted.

Potato   2 cups grated
Salt   ½ teaspoon
Egg   1, beaten
Onion   ¼ cup grated
Medium onion   1, chopped
Medium garlic cloves   2, crushed
Butter   3 to 4 tablespoons
Mushrooms   ¼ pound, thinly sliced
Medium cauliflower   1, broken into small flowerets
Thyme   ½ teaspoon crushed
Basil   ½ teaspoon crushed
Salt   to taste
Cheddar cheese   1 to 1½ cups grated
Eggs   2, beaten
Milk   ¼ cup
Pepper   to taste
Paprika   garnish

1. Preheat oven to 400°.
2. Salt freshly grated potato and leave in colander to drain for 10 minutes. Squeeze out excess liquid (reserve for soup stock, if desired). Combine potatoes, ½ teaspoon salt, 1 beaten egg, and ¼ cup grated onion and pat into a well-oiled pie pan. With lightly floured fingers, build up the sides of the crust until you have an even shell.
3. Bake crust 40 to 45 minutes, until lightly browned. Brush with oil after the first 30 minutes to crisp.
4. Sauté 1 onion and garlic in butter until onion is transparent (about 3 minutes). Add mushrooms and sauté 3 to 5 minutes more. Add cauliflower and seasonings, cover, and cook for 10 minutes, stirring occasionally.
5. Sprinkle half of grated cheese into baked crust. Add sautéed vegetables, then remaining cheese. Combine 2 beaten eggs and milk and pour over.
6. Dust with pepper and paprika and bake for 35 to 40 minutes until custard is set. Serve at once.

Toadiccelli's Ravioli
Serves 4

We were quite surprised to find this recipe for ravioli stuffed with, guess what . . . potatoes! If you have the equipment for making ravioli, try this filling and sauce combination.

Medium potatoes 2
Medium onion 1, minced
Olive oil 3 tablespoons
Parsley 1 cup minced
Eggs 2
Freshly grated nutmeg to taste
Salt and pepper to taste
Peeled tomatoes 16-ounce can, chopped
Butter 2 tablespoons
Basil ¼ teaspoon (optional)
Salt and pepper to taste
Grated romano cheese to taste

1. Boil potatoes in their skins in salted water until tender. Drain, peel, and mash roughly. Place in a large bowl.
2. Sauté minced onion in olive oil until tender. Stir in parsley, then pour mixture into mashed potatoes. Add eggs, nutmeg, salt, and pepper and beat or process well to ensure a smooth consistency. Set aside.
3. Prepare pasta according to instructions on ravioli maker, stuff with potato mixture, and cook.
4. Combine tomatoes, butter, basil, salt, and pepper in a small skillet and simmer for a few minutes so flavors combine and sauce reduces slightly. Spoon over ravioli and sprinkle with romano cheese. Serve immediately.

Variation: For a little spice, cook and mince 2 italian sausages and add to the potato filling.

Italian Spinach and Potato Roulade
Serves 6 to 8

This is one of the best vegetarian entrées we can think of—and in good part that's because it came from Anna Thomas's Vegetarian Epicure *cookbook. We've made a few minor changes here and there, but it remains a dish that requires little innovation.*

Medium potatoes   4 to 6
Eggs   2
Egg yolk   1
Salt   1½ teaspoons
Nutmeg   ⅛ teaspoon
Flour   2 to 2½ cups
Spinach Filling
Parmesan   1½ cups grated
Butter   1 cup, melted
Mushrooms   ¾ pound, sliced

1.   Boil potatoes until tender; peel and mash in a large bowl. Beat eggs and egg yolk and stir into potatoes along with salt and nutmeg. Stir in about 2 cups flour and begin working the dough by hand until smooth. (Be sure to flour your hands adequately so they don't stick to the dough.) Work in as much flour as necessary to form a dough stiff enough to hold its shape in a ball.
2.   Sprinkle a large sheet of waxed paper with a generous amount of flour and roll dough out in an even 11- by 13-inch rectangle. Keep dough dusted with flour to prevent sticking.
3.   Prepare Spinach Filling according to directions. Spread filling over dough, leaving a 2-inch border on 1 of the 13-inch sides and a 1-inch border on the 3 remaining sides. Sprinkle ½ cup parmesan over filling. Starting with the long side that has the 1-inch border, roll the dough up over the filling, peeling back the waxed paper as you go. Securely pinch together the seam and ends so that none of the filling can squeeze out.
4.   Wrap the entire roulade in cheesecloth, 2 or 3 layers thick and long enough to extend past both ends of the roulade by several inches. Tie

the cheesecloth with string at the ends, and tie another strip of cheese-cloth, about 3 inches wide, around the middle of the roulade.

5. Place the roulade in a large, fairly deep pan, such as a roasting pan, and cover it with boiling salted water. Simmer the roulade for 50 minutes, turning it over once, halfway through.

6. Lift out roulade and let it rest for a couple of minutes, then carefully remove cheesecloth; use a sharp knife to help peel away cheesecloth if it should stick.

7. Melt butter; add mushrooms and cook for 2 to 3 minutes, until mushroom juices combine with butter.

8. Cut roulade into ¾-inch slices and serve them immediately, drenched with mushroom sauce and sprinkled liberally with remaining parmesan.

Note: If you wish to microwave the roulade, place it in a large casserole dish, pour boiling water over it, and microwave on high heat for 15 minutes on each side.

Spinach Filling

Fresh spinach   2 pounds
Butter   3 tablespoons
Large onion   1, chopped
Garlic clove   2, minced
White wine vinegar   1½ tablespoons
Salt   ½ teaspoon
Oregano   ¼ teaspoon
Nutmeg   pinch

1. Wash spinach carefully and cook, covered, in water that clings to the leaves, until they are wilted. Squeeze out excess moisture and finely chop spinach.

2. Melt butter in a medium-sized skillet and sauté onions and garlic until golden. Stir in chopped spinach, vinegar, salt, oregano, and nutmeg. Stir and continue cooking for a few minutes, until mixture is thick but still moist. Taste, and correct seasoning if necessary.

Potato-Zucchini Casserole
Serves 4 to 6

The yogurt and cheddar custard makes this vegetable combination exceedingly good.

Yogurt 2 cups
Vegetable oil ¼ cup
Cheddar cheese 1½ cups grated
Paprika ½ to 1 teaspoon
Egg 1, beaten
Green onions 3 to 4, sliced
Medium potatoes 4, boiled, peeled, and cubed
Salt and pepper to taste
Zucchini 4 cups sliced
Fine bread crumbs ¼ to ½ cup
Parmesan cheese ¼ to ½ cup grated
Butter 2 tablespoons

1. Preheat oven to 375°.
2. Combine yogurt, oil, and cheddar in a saucepan and simmer slowly until cheese melts. Add paprika, blend, and remove from heat. Stir in beaten egg and green onions. Set aside.
3. Place potato cubes in bottom of a 2½-quart baking dish. Salt and pepper to taste. Top with overlapping zucchini slices.
4. Pour cheese mixture over all. Sprinkle with bread crumbs, parmesan, and dots of butter.
5. Bake for about 45 minutes.

Potato and Zucchini Torta
Serves 4

This is an inviting, quichelike dish, perfect for brunch.

Small new potatoes 6
Zucchini 1 pound
Garlic clove 1, halved
Butter 1 tablespoon
Olive oil 2 tablespoons
Salt and pepper to taste
Eggs 4
Romano cheese ¼ to ½ cup grated
Medium tomatoes (canned or fresh) 2
Parsley ¼ cup chopped

1. Preheat oven to 375°.
2. Drop potatoes into boiling water to cover, and cook for 10 minutes. Drain, rinse with cold water, peel, and dice.
3. Wash and trim zucchini. Grate it or chop in a food processor. Rub a deep 9-inch pie or quiche dish with garlic pieces, then butter it with 1 tablespoon butter.
4. Heat oil in skillet and over low heat gently cook potatoes with garlic cloves used earlier (mince first) until golden. Add zucchini, salt, and pepper and cook for 1 minute. Remove pan from heat.
5. Break eggs into a mixing bowl and beat to mix. Add grated cheese. Use a slotted spoon to add potatoes and zucchini to eggs. Leave the oil in skillet.
6. Pour mixture into buttered pan. Bake for 20 to 25 minutes, until eggs are baked and puffed up.
7. While torta is baking, blanch and peel tomatoes (if fresh), dice them, and mix with parsley. Sauté mixture in oil remaining in skillet until tomatoes are soft. (If using canned tomatoes, mix with parsley and simmer until saucelike consistency.)
8. Cut torta into wedges to serve, and garnish each serving with a spoonful of tomato mixture. This can be served hot or cold.

Potato and Zucchini Omelets
Serves 4

Potatoes, zucchini, and onions seasoned with herbs and sour cream make for a filling, full-flavored omelet.

Potatoes   1 cup diced
Zucchini   1 cup diced
Butter   3 tablespoons
Olive oil   2 tablespoons
Small onion   1, chopped
Dill weed   ¼ teaspoon (optional)
Dried basil   ¼ teaspoon crushed
Cayenne   pinch or
   Dried red pepper   ¼ teaspoon crushed
Salt and pepper   to taste
Eggs   6 to 8, room temperature
Sour cream   to taste

1. Cook diced potato in boiling salted water for about 5 minutes. Drain and set aside. Cook zucchini in boiling water for about 3 minutes. Drain and set aside.
2. Heat 1 tablespoon butter and olive oil in medium-sized skillet until melted, add chopped onions, and sauté until onions are just turning color. Add precooked potatoes and zucchini and seasonings. Cook mixture over moderate heat until vegetables are tender. Correct seasoning.
3. Make 2 medium or 4 individual omelets, sautéing in remaining butter and filling with vegetable mixture. Slide onto heated plates and serve immediately with sour cream.

Note: Here are some suggestions that will make omelets seem less intimidating and that ensure good results:

(1) Be sure to prepare filling before making omelet so that the omelet can be prepared with no delay.

(2) The omelet pan you use should be a proper size and shape. An omelet for 2 people can be prepared in an 8-inch pan made of heavy metal, with rounded, slanting sides. (A straight-edged pan is good for scrambled eggs, but can make a mess of a well-shaped omelet.)

(3) When you first pour the eggs into your heated pan with melted butter, give them a swirl with a whisk. As the egg mixture begins to set, use a spatula to lift the edges of the omelet so that the uncooked eggs on top can run underneath. (Continue to do this until there is no more runny egg.)

(4) While the eggs are still somewhat moist on top, slide the omelet toward the pan's handle, spread the filling mixture on it, and fold it in half.

Baked
Goods
and Desserts_____

Potato Rolls
Makes 2 dozen

Everyone loves these chewy rolls. The potato adds a savory richness to the flavor of an altogether splendid roll.

Small potato 1, peeled and halved
Dry yeast ¼-ounce packet
Sugar 2 teaspoons
Flour 3 cups
Unsalted butter 2 tablespoons
Salt 1½ teaspoons
Egg 1, lightly beaten
Salt ½ teaspoon
Poppy seeds, sesame seeds, celery seeds, or coarse salt (optional)

1. Cook potato in hot water to cover until soft. Remove from heat and let stand. When water has cooled to about 110°, transfer 1 cup to a small bowl. Add yeast and sugar and let stand in warm place for about 10 minutes, until mixture is foamy. Oil a large bowl and set aside.
2. Process potato in food processor. Add 2½ cups flour, butter, and 1½ teaspoons salt and mix. (Alternately, you can mash potato and mix ingredients by hand.) Pour in yeast mixture and add enough flour to make dough sticky and soft, but not wet. Mix until dough pulls away from bowl and is smooth and elastic.
3. Place dough in oiled bowl and turn to coat all surfaces. Cover and let stand in a warm area free of drafts until doubled in size, about 1 hour.
4. Generously grease two 12-cup or three 8-cup muffin tins and enough plastic wrap to cover. Punch dough to release gases and transfer to a lightly floured board. Divide dough in half, then divide each half into 12 equal pieces, using a sharp knife. Roll each piece into a smooth ball and pinch the bottom. Place in muffin tins with pinched sides down. Cover with plastic wrap, greased side touching dough. Let stand another hour, until doubled. Remove plastic. Fifteen minutes before baking, preheat oven to 400°.
5. Mix egg and ½ teaspoon salt and brush onto tops of rolls. Sprinkle with poppy seeds, if desired, and bake for 10 minutes. Reduce heat to 350° and continue baking 10 to 12 minutes more, until rolls are lightly browned. Remove from pans and cool on racks.

Rich Potato Rolls
Makes about 4 dozen small

These rolls may look like a lot of work at first glance, but don't be intimidated. With a short stint one evening and an average mixing time the next day, you have several days worth of refrigerated rolls that can be freshly baked each time. And the result is "ooh and ahh" with every bite.

Dry active yeast   ¼-ounce packet or
    Yeast cake   1
Lukewarm water   1 cup
Mashed potatoes   1 cup, unseasoned
Sugar   1 cup
Eggs   4
Butter   ½ cup, softened
Salt   1 teaspoon
Unbleached flour   5 to 6 cups

1. In large mixing bowl soften yeast in water. Stir in potatoes and sugar; stir until sugar is dissolved. Cover with a towel and let stand in a warm place overnight.
2. Add eggs, softened butter, and salt to potato mixture and beat well.
3. Stir in about 3 cups flour to make a stiff dough that is difficult to stir. Then, with your hands, mix in another 2 to 3 cups flour to make a soft, light dough. (Be careful not to add any more flour than necessary.)
4. Turn dough out onto floured surface and roll with floured rolling pin until about ½ inch thick. Cut out small rounds with floured cookie cutter. Place rounds 1 inch apart on buttered baking sheets. (Rolls can be refrigerated at this point.)
5. Cover rolls with a towel and let rise at room temperature until doubled, about 2 hours.
6. Bake rolls in preheated 400° oven for 10 minutes or until just lightly tinged with brown. Serve warm.

Note: To refrigerate rolls for future use, place precut rolls covered with buttered wax paper in refrigerator. After removing rolls from refrigerator, allow 3 hours rising time. Bake as above.

Potato Oatmeal Bread
Makes 2 loaves

This is a chewy, peasant-type bread, similar to sourdough in texture. You can make crusty dinner rolls from the same recipe.

Large potato   1, peeled and cut into chunks
Potato water   ½ cup
Milk   1½ cups
Butter   1½ tablespoons
Dry active yeast   ¼-ounce packet
Ground ginger   ¼ teaspoon
Sugar   4 teaspoons
Salt   1 tablespoon
Flour   5½ to 6 cups
Rolled oats   1 cup uncooked

1. Boil potato in small amount of unsalted water until soft. Pour off water, reserving ½ cup of it, and mash potato with a little of milk and butter until smooth.
2. Put potato water in small bowl; when cooled to lukewarm, sprinkle with yeast, ginger, and 1 teaspoon of sugar.
3. Scald remaining milk with rest of butter, salt, and sugar. As it cools, begin stirring gradually into mashed potato until very smooth.
4. When this mixture is somewhat cooled and yeast mixture is foamy, mix them together in a large bowl and add 4 cups flour, plus 1 cup oats. Stir vigorously with wooden spoon. Add more flour, stirring until dough can no longer be stirred with a spoon.
5. Turn dough out on a well-floured board and knead for 10 to 15 minutes, adding flour as needed, until dough is elastic and smooth. (Beware of adding too much flour. If dough is getting quite stiff, but still sticking, wash your hands and rub them with butter, as well as the board. This will prevent bread from becoming too dry from too much flour.) Place dough in a large, buttered bowl, turn it over once or twice so that it is buttered on all surfaces, and cover with a towel. Set aside in a warm place to rise until doubled in size; this should take 1½ to 2 hours.
6. Punch it down and let rise again, about 1 hour. Knead it down, divide into 2 parts, and form loaves. (To make dinner rolls instead of bread, form dough into a long roll about 2 inches in diameter. Cut across in pieces about 3 inches long.) Place loaves in buttered loaf pans (dinner

rolls on buttered cookie sheet), cover again with towel, and let rise about 30 minutes, or until almost double.

7. Put into preheated 400° oven. Turn heat down to 350° after 10 minutes and bake another 30 to 35 minutes.

Potato Bread
Makes 2 loaves

Soft-textured and moist, potato bread is a traditional American favorite.

Active dry yeast ¼-ounce packet
Sugar 1 tablespoon
Warm potato water ¼ cup
Butter ¼ cup, room temperature
Salt 1 tablespoon
Warm potato water ¾ cup combined with
   Warm milk ¾ cup or
   Warm potato water 1½ cups
Mashed potatoes ¾ cup
Flour 5½ to 6 cups

1. Proof yeast and sugar in the ¼ cup warm potato water.
2. In a large mixing bowl combine butter, salt, and liquids. Stir to melt butter. Add potatoes, stir in yeast mixture, and add enough flour to make a stiff dough.
3. Turn out on a floured board and knead until dough is no longer sticky, about 10 minutes. Place in a buttered bowl and roll dough around until coated with butter. Cover, and allow to rise until doubled in bulk, 1½ to 2 hours.
4. Punch down and knead briefly. Cover, and allow to rise again about 30 minutes.
5. Place on a floured board and divide into 2 parts. Mold into balls. Cover dough and let it rest 15 minutes. Shape into loaves and place in well-buttered 8½- by 4½-inch bread pans. Cover, and allow to rise in a warm place until dough appears above top of pans.
6. Dust loaves with flour. Bake at 400° 20 minutes, then reduce heat to 350°. Bake another 25 to 35 minutes, or until brown and hollow-sounding when tapped. Transfer immediately to a rack to cool.

Potato Rye Bread with Fruit
Makes 1 loaf

If you like Boston brown bread, we think you'll like this even better. It's a dense, slightly sweet bread, which should be thinly sliced and served with butter or cream cheese. You can refrigerate it for up to two weeks.

Active dry yeast   ¼-ounce packet
Warm potato water   ½ cup
Warm mashed potatoes   1 cup
Molasses   ¼ cup
Whole wheat flour   about 2 cups
Medium or dark rye flour   1¼ cups
Salt   1 teaspoon
Wheat germ   ¼ cup
Prunes   ⅓ cup chopped
Raisins   ⅓ cup
Currants   ⅓ cup
Walnuts   ⅓ cup chopped
Egg yolk   1
Water   1 tablespoon

1. Dissolve yeast in warm potato water (about 85°); set aside until foamy (about 10 minutes).
2. Stir mixture into mashed potatoes in a large bowl. Add molasses and 1 cup of whole wheat flour and blend well. Cover bowl with a light towel and put away in a warm, draft-free place for 1½ hours to let sponge rise.
3. Stir down the sponge. Combine rye flour and salt, then blend in, along with wheat germ, fruit, and nuts (using hands if necessary).
4. Turn dough out onto heavily floured surface and knead in as much more of the whole wheat flour as is necessary to make a manageable dough. Continue kneading dough until it feels elastic and springs back when pushed down.
5. Form dough into a ball and put in a large, lightly buttered bowl. Turn it over once, cover bowl with a towel, and put it aside in a warm place for 1½ hours, or until dough has risen to about twice its former size.
6. Punch dough down, form a ball again, and let dough rise again for about 45 minutes.
7. Punch dough down, form into a ball, and place, smooth side up, on a buttered baking sheet. Cover with a light towel and let rise for 45 minutes.
8. Brush loaf with glaze made of beaten egg yolk and water and bake in a preheated oven at 375° for 1 hour.
9. Allow loaf to cool before slicing.

Caraway Potato Bread
Makes 1 large round loaf

This bread is incredibly moist and abundantly seasoned. A great accompaniment for a soup and salad dinner.

Warm water ¼ cup (about 110°)
Active dry yeast ¼-ounce packet
Sugar 1½ tablespoons
Mashed potatoes 1 cup
Butter 2 tablespoons, softened
Evaporated milk 6½-ounce can
Dried minced onion 1 tablespoon
Caraway seeds 2 teaspoons
Garlic salt 1 teaspoon
Celery salt 1 teaspoon
Egg 1
Flour 3 to 3½ cups

1. In a small bowl, combine water, yeast, and sugar; let stand until foamy (about 10 minutes).
2. Place mashed potatoes in a large bowl. Beat in butter; then gradually beat in evaporated milk until blended. Add onion, caraway seeds, garlic salt, celery salt, egg, yeast mixture, and 2 cups of flour; beat until blended.
3. Gradually stir in 1 additional cup flour. Turn dough out onto a heavily floured board. Knead dough until smooth and elastic (about 10 minutes), adding remaining flour to board as necessary to prevent sticking.
4. Place dough in a greased bowl, turning to grease top. Cover and let rise in a warm place until doubled in size (about 1½ to 2 hours).
5. Punch dough down and knead briefly to release air bubbles. Shape into a round and place in a greased 2-quart casserole or soufflé dish or on a greased cookie sheet. Cover and let rise in a warm place until almost doubled (about 40 minutes).
6. Bake, uncovered, in a 350° oven for about 50 minutes or until loaf is richly browned on top and sounds hollow when tapped. Turn loaf out onto a wire rack to cool thoroughly before slicing.

Potato Raisin Bread
Makes 2 loaves

This slightly sweet potato bread is delicious just sliced but even better lightly toasted with butter.

Mashed potato   ¼ cup
Potato water   1 cup
Flour   4 to 5 cups
Sugar   ½ cup
Salt   1 teaspoon
Dry yeast   two ¼-ounce packets
Butter   ½ cup
Eggs   2
Raisins   1 cup

1. Prepare mashed potatoes, reserving liquid. Set aside.
2. Combine 1½ cups flour, sugar, salt, and yeast in small bowl. Set aside.
3. Heat potato water with butter until butter is melted. Cool to lukewarm. Pour into a large bowl, then stir in flour mixture. Beat with electric mixer at medium speed for 2 minutes.
4. Add eggs, mashed potato, and another 1 to 1½ cups flour. Beat at high speed for an additional 2 minutes.
5. Stir in raisins and enough flour to make a soft dough. Turn out onto a floured board and knead until smooth and elastic (about 8 minutes), adding flour as necessary.
6. Place in buttered bowl and rotate to coat dough with butter. Cover and let rise in a warm place until doubled, 1 to 1½ hours.
7. Punch down, knead briefly, and shape into loaves. Place dough in greased loaf pans, cover, and let rise again until nearly doubled.
8. Bake at 350° for 35 to 40 minutes. Turn out on racks to cool.

Quick Potato Doughnuts
Makes 30 to 36

These doughnuts are breadlike in consistency, not too sweet. Perfect with coffee for a finale to brunch.

Eggs 2
Sugar ⅔ cup
Potatoes 1 cup freshly riced or mashed
Buttermilk 1 cup
Butter 2 tablespoons, melted
Flour 4 cups presifted
Baking powder 2 teaspoons
Baking soda 1 teaspoon
Salt ⅔ teaspoon
Cinnamon or nutmeg ¼ to ½ teaspoon
Oil for deep frying
Powdered sugar or sugar and cinnamon garnish (optional)

1. Beat eggs well. Slowly add ⅔ cup sugar, beating constantly. Stir in freshly prepared potatoes, buttermilk, and melted butter.
2. Sift flour with baking powder, soda, salt, and cinnamon.
3. Add enough of flour to potato mixture to make a soft dough. Chill dough for about 1 hour or until it is easy to handle.
4. On a lightly floured board, roll or pat dough to about ½-inch thickness. Cut with a well-floured double cutter or 2 sizes of biscuit cutters (about 2½ inches outer diameter, 1 inch inner). Allow dough to dry 10 to 12 minutes (doughnuts will absorb less fat).
5. Preheat deep fryer to 370°. Slide doughnuts, 1 at a time, into hot oil, using a pancake turner that has been dipped in oil. Cook each doughnut about 3 minutes, turning as soon as it is golden brown on 1 side.
6. Remove with strainer or tongs and drain on paper toweling. Sprinkle with powdered sugar if desired.

Chocolate Potato Cake with Mother's Fudge Frosting
Serves 10 to 12

Chocolate potato cake is really one of the staples of turn-of-the-century American cookbooks. Cooks of that period added potatoes to a cake for a practical reason: they made up for whatever flour might be lacking or difficult to obtain. The even better reason for using potatoes was that they made for a moist cake that lasted for several days. This version is typical of those early cakes and is made even richer and more sinful with the addition of a fudge frosting.

Unsweetened chocolate   4 squares (4 ounces)
Butter   ½ cup softened
Sugar   2 cups
Large eggs   4
Vanilla   1 teaspoon
Flour   2 cups
Baking soda   1 teaspoon
Baking powder   1 tablespoon
Salt   1 teaspoon
Cold mashed potatoes   1 cup
Buttermilk   ¾ cup
Fudge Frosting

1. Preheat oven to 350°.
2. Melt chocolate in double boiler over hot water and cool.
3. Cream butter, add sugar, and beat until fluffy. Add eggs and vanilla

and beat at medium speed with electric mixer until well blended.

4. Blend chocolate into butter mixture.
5. Sift together dry ingredients and add to mixture. Beat for 4 minutes at medium speed.
6. Add mashed potatoes and beat until blended, about 1 to 2 minutes. Pour in buttermilk and beat for an additional minute.
7. Pour batter into buttered 9- by 13-inch baking pan and bake for 40 to 45 minutes, or until a toothpick pushed into center emerges clean. Cool on wire rack and frost when cooled.

Mother's Fudge Frosting
Makes 1 cup

This is a delicious, almost foolproof recipe for frosting that can even serve as plain old fudge on a quiet, rainy day.

Butter   ½ cup
Cocoa   4 tablespoons
Cream or evaporated milk   6 tablespoons
Powdered sugar   1 pound box

1. Place first 3 ingredients in a heavy-bottomed saucepan over medium-low heat, stirring constantly until completely melted and blended.
2. Remove from heat and add sifted sugar. Stir until frosting has a dull sheen and spoon over cake immediately, spreading with a knife until evenly distributed.

Potato Sponge Cake with Chantilly Filling
Serves 4 to 6

We love the fine texture and delicate flavor of this cake.

Egg yolks   6
Egg   1
Sugar   1½ cups
Lemon juice   1½ tablespoons
Lemon rind   2 teaspoons grated
Potato starch flour   ¾ cup sifted
Cream of tartar   ¼ teaspoon
Salt   dash
Egg whites   6
Chantilly Filling

1. Preheat oven to 350°.
2. Beat the 6 egg yolks and 1 whole egg until thick.
3. Gradually add 1 cup sugar. Add lemon juice and lemon rind and beat well. Gradually add potato starch flour and beat until well blended.
4. Add cream of tartar and salt to egg whites. Beat until very foamy. Slowly add remaining ½ cup sugar, beating until egg whites form stiff peaks. Fold gently, but thoroughly into egg yolk mixture with rapid strokes.
5. Pour into an ungreased 10-inch tube pan and bake for about 55 minutes or until cake springs back when touched gently with finger.
6. Invert tube pan so that the cake itself does not touch anything. (Use inverted funnel if center tube of pan is not long enough.) Leave cake "hanging" until cooled (1 to 1½ hours) before removing.
7. Slice cake carefully in half horizontally and coat with a third to a half of the Chantilly Filling.
8. Join halves of cake and coat top (and sides if desired) with remaining filling.

Chantilly Filling
Makes 2 cups

Cream   1 cup, whipped
Powdered sugar   1 to 3 tablespoons
Vanilla   ½ teaspoon
Almonds, walnuts, or pecans   ½ cup blanched and slivered or
    Marmalade or jam   ½ cup or
    Fresh berries or sliced fruit   ¾ cup

1.   Whip cream until stiff. Fold in sugar and vanilla.
2.   Add chosen flavoring and blend well.

Potato-Molasses Drops
Makes about 50

If you love gingerbready, chewy cakes and cookies, these drops may be just what you've been looking for. One of the things we like best about this sweet is that it is not too sweet.

Flour   2 cups
Baking soda   ½ teaspoon
Baking powder   2 teaspoons
Ginger   ½ teaspoon
Cinnamon   ½ teaspoon
Salt   ½ teaspoon
Dark molasses   ½ cup
Butter   ½ cup
Brown sugar   ⅓ cup
Mashed potatoes   1½ cups
Walnuts   1 cup chopped
Powdered sugar

1.   Preheat oven to 375°.
2.   Sift together first 6 ingredients and set aside.
3.   Combine molasses and butter in top of double boiler and place over hot water, beating until heated through and butter is melted.
4.   Add sifted dry ingredients and brown sugar and mix well. Beat in potatoes until mixture is smooth and well blended. Stir in walnuts.
5.   Drop from a teaspoon onto buttered cookie sheet and bake for 10 minutes. Remove from oven, sprinkle with powdered sugar, and cool.

Fudgy Potato Drops
Makes 6 dozen

The name of this recipe may well frighten the less adventurous potato fan, but the moist, chocolate result will help even the most timid overcome all hesitation.

Solid vegetable shortening   ¼ cup
Brown sugar   1 cup firmly packed
Cold mashed potatoes   ½ cup
Egg   1
Unsweetened chocolate   2 ounces, melted
Vanilla   1 teaspoon
Flour   1½ cups
Salt   ½ teaspoon
Baking soda   ½ teaspoon
Buttermilk   ¾ cup
Pecans   ½ cup chopped
Fudge Frosting
Toasted pecan halves   garnish (optional)

1. Preheat oven to 400°.
2. Grease baking sheets. Cream shortening with sugar in large mixing bowl. Beat in potatoes, egg, chocolate, and vanilla and mix thoroughly.
3. Sift flour, salt, and baking soda. Blend into potato mixture alternately with buttermilk. Stir in chopped pecans.
4. Drop dough onto prepared sheets by heaping teaspoons, spacing 2 inches apart. Bake until browned, about 6 to 8 minutes.
5. Cool on rack 5 minutes. Spread 1½ teaspoons frosting over each cookie while warm. Press pecan half into top.

Fudge Frosting
Makes 1½ cups

Butter 6 tablespoons
Unsweetened chocolate 1½ ounces
Milk 4½ tablespoons, room temperature
Powdered sugar 3 cups
Vanilla ¾ teaspoon

1. Melt butter and chocolate in small saucepan over low heat. Transfer to bowl.
2. Add milk and stir until smooth. Beat in sugar and vanilla and blend thoroughly.
3. Cover and set aside.

Swedish Butter Cookies
Makes 6 dozen

These are simple to prepare and simply wonderful.

Butter 1 cup
Sugar 1 cup
Egg 1
Vanilla 1 teaspoon
Flour 1 cup
Potato starch flour 1 cup

1. Cream butter; add sugar and cream again. Beat in egg and vanilla.
2. Sift flour and potato starch flour together and add to creamed mixture, blending thoroughly. Chill dough for at least 2 hours.
3. Preheat oven to 375°.
4. Form dough into small rounds, place on lightly buttered cookie sheet, and flatten with fork or spoon back. Bake for 8 to 10 minutes, until very lightly browned.

Norwegian Dalesman Cakes
Makes 25 to 30 cookies

A nice, light, decadent cookie with whipped cream and chopped almonds.

Butter   ½ cup
Sugar   ½ cup
Cream   ½ cup, whipped
Potato starch flour   ½ cup
Flour   1 cup
Blanched almonds   ¾ cup minced
Vanilla   ½ teaspoon

1.   Preheat oven to 350°.
2.   Cream butter until light and fluffy. Beat in sugar until mixture whitens. Beat in whipped cream.
3.   Stir in potato starch flour, flour, almonds, and vanilla. Combine well.
4.   Drop dough by teaspoonfuls onto lightly greased cookie sheets. Bake for 10 to 12 minutes, or until golden brown.

Potato "Marzipan" Tarts
Makes 8 to 16

Kathy Sugawara Rossol gave us this recipe for a family holiday favorite. It is delicate and buttery and can stand the test of matching all your other holiday sweets.

Sugar   ⅓ cup
Butter   ½ cup
Flour   1⅔ cups
Egg   1
Cream or whole milk   1 teaspoon
Almonds   12
Potatoes   4, boiled and mashed
Sugar   1 cup
Egg   1
Butter   ½ cup
Almond extract   1 teaspoon

1. Preheat oven to 375°.
2. Cream ⅓ cup sugar and ½ cup butter together until fluffy. Add flour, 1 egg, and then cream and mix thoroughly. Coat insides of buttered tart tins with dough (the thinner the layer of dough, the lighter the tart will be).
3. Scald almonds in boiling water, peel, and grind. Add almonds to potatoes along with 1 cup sugar and 1 egg and mix well. Add ½ cup butter and almond extract and mix.
4. Fill coated tart tins half full with filling. Bake 15 to 20 minutes until lightly browned. Cool briefly in tins, then remove and finish cooling on rack.

Variation: If you are a chocolate fan, just add 1½ ounces of melted, cooled unsweetened chocolate to the dough mixture that lines the tart tins. For true almond lovers, it may overwhelm the marzipan effect, but for others it will be an unexpected treat.

German Honey Potato Custard
Serves 4

This is a homey dessert, like bread or rice pudding, delicately flavored with honey and lemon.

Warm mashed potatoes 1 cup
Butter 2 tablespoons (room temperature)
Honey ¼ to ⅓ cup
Vanilla ¼ teaspoon
Salt pinch
Eggs 2, separated
Milk or half-and-half ⅓ cup
Lemon juice from ½ lemon
Lemon peel grated, from ½ lemon
Raisins ¼ cup (optional)
Nutmeg garnish

1. Preheat oven to 350°.
2. Combine mashed potatoes, butter, honey, vanilla, and salt in a mixing bowl. Blend until creamy.
3. In separate bowl, stir egg yolks, milk, lemon juice, and lemon peel together. Add to potato mixture and beat until well blended. Stir in raisins if desired.
4. Beat egg whites until stiff, then fold into custard. Pour into a well-greased baking dish and bake for about 30 minutes or until custard has set and is golden around the edges. Dust with nutmeg and serve warm or cold.

Pioneer Potato Candy
Makes about 8 dozen

You'll be amazed, as we were, at how delicious this traditional fondant is. With the modern addition of a chocolate and nut coating, these are very much like Mountain Bars!

Warm mashed potatoes   1 cup, unseasoned
Salt   ½ teaspoon
Vanilla   2 teaspoons
Powdered sugar*   2 pounds
Dipping chocolate or semisweet chocolate   1 pound
Salted peanuts   ⅔ cup ground

1. Combine potatoes, salt, and vanilla in a 4-quart mixing bowl. Sift powdered sugar over potatoes, stirring and adding about 1 cup at a time. Mixture will liquefy when first sugar is added, then gradually begin to thicken. When it becomes the consistency of stiff dough, knead it even though not all sugar may have been added.
2. After kneading, cover with a damp cloth; chill until a small spoonful can be rolled into a ball.
3. Shape in small ½-inch balls. Dip balls in chocolate that has been melted in double boiler (being sure to leave chocolate over hot water so that it won't solidify), then roll in peanuts.

* The amount of powdered sugar needed will vary according to the water content of the potatoes used.

U.S. and Metric Measurements

Approximate conversion formulas are given below for commonly used U.S. and metric kitchen measurements.

Teaspoons	x	5	= milliliters
Tablespoons	x	15	= milliliters
Fluid ounces	x	30	= milliliters
Fluid ounces	x	0.03	= liters
Cups	x	240	= milliliters
Cups	x	0.24	= liters
Pints	x	0.47	= liters
Dry pints	x	0.55	= liters
Quarts	x	0.95	= liters
Dry quarts	x	1.1	= liters
Gallons	x	3.8	= liters
Ounces	x	28	= grams
Ounces	x	0.028	= kilograms
Pounds	x	454	= grams
Pounds	x	0.45	= kilograms
Milliliters	x	0.2	= teaspoons
Milliliters	x	0.07	= tablespoons
Milliliters	x	0.034	= fluid ounces
Milliliters	x	0.004	= cups
Liters	x	34	= fluid ounces
Liters	x	4.2	= cups
Liters	x	2.1	= pints
Liters	x	1.82	= dry pints
Liters	x	1.06	= quarts
Liters	x	0.91	= dry quarts
Liters	x	0.26	= gallons
Grams	x	0.035	= ounces
Grams	x	0.002	= pounds
Kilograms	x	35	= ounces
Kilograms	x	2.2	= pounds

Temperature Equivalents

Fahrenheit	− 32	× 5	÷ 9	= Celsius
Celsius	× 9	÷ 5	+ 32	= Fahrenheit

U.S. Equivalents

1 teaspoon	= ⅓ tablespoon
1 tablespoon	= 3 teaspoons
2 tablespoons	= 1 fluid ounce
4 tablespoons	= ¼ cup or 2 ounces
5⅓ tablespoons	= ⅓ cup or 2⅔ ounces
8 tablespoons	= ½ cup or 4 ounces
16 tablespoons	= 1 cup or 8 ounces
⅜ cup	= ¼ cup plus 2 tablespoons
⅝ cup	= ½ cup plus 2 tablespoons
⅞ cup	= ¾ cup plus 2 tablespoons
1 cup	= ½ pint or 8 fluid ounces
2 cups	= 1 pint or 16 fluid ounces
1 liquid quart	= 2 pints or 4 cups
1 liquid gallon	= 4 quarts

Metric Equivalents

1 milliliter	= 0.001 liter
1 liter	= 1000 milliliters
1 milligram	= 0.001 gram
1 gram	= 1000 milligrams
1 kilogram	= 1000 grams

Index

Other Cookbooks from Pacific Search Press

The Apple Cookbook by Kyle D. Fulwiler
Asparagus: The Sparrowgrass Cookbook by Autumn Stanley
The Bean Cookbook: Dry Legume Cookery by Norma S. Upson
The Berry Cookbook by Kyle D. Fulwiler
Bone Appétit! Natural Foods for Pets by Frances Sheridan Goulart
Canning and Preserving without Sugar by Norma M. MacRae, R.D.
The Carrot Cookbook by Ann Saling
The Crawfish Cookbook by Norma S. Upson
The Dogfish Cookbook by Russ Mohney
The Eggplant Cookbook by Norma S. Upson
A Fish Feast by Charlotte Wright
Food 101: A Student Guide to Quick and Easy Cooking by Cathy Smith
The Green Tomato Cookbook by Paula Simmons
Mushrooms 'n Bean Sprouts: A First Step for Would-be Vegetarians by
     Norma M. MacRae, R.D.
My Secret Cookbook by Paula Simmons
The Natural Fast Food Cookbook by Gail L. Worstman
The Natural Fruit Cookbook by Gail L. Worstman
Rhubarb Renaissance: A Cookbook by Ann Saling
Roots & Tubers: A Vegetable Cookbook by Kyle D. Fulwiler
The Salmon Cookbook by Jerry Dennon
Starchild & Holahan's Seafood Cookbook by Adam Starchild and James
     Holahan
Warm & Tasty: The Wood Heat Stove Cookbook by Margaret Byrd
     Adams
The Whole Grain Bake Book by Gail L. Worstman
Wild Mushroom Recipes by Puget Sound Mycological Society
The Zucchini Cookbook (3d Ed. Revised & Enlarged) by Paula
     Simmons